THE ZERO-WASTE KITCHEN

A Comprehensive Guide to Transforming Your Cooking Space into an Eco-friendly Haven

Colton Drexel

DISCLAIMER

The book is intended for informational and educational purposes only. The contents of this book are the opinions of the author and are not intended to serve as a substitute for professional advice, diagnosis, or treatment.

The author and publisher have made every effort to ensure that the information provided in this book is accurate and useful, but they accept no responsibility for any errors or omissions, or any outcomes related to the use of this information. The book does not offer legal, psychological, or other professional advice. If professional assistance is required, the services of a competent professional should be sought.

Any case studies, examples, illustrations, or quotes used in this book are provided as examples only and should not be considered as advice that would apply to all individuals or all situations. The effectiveness of the strategies discussed may vary based on the specific circumstances of the reader.

The author and publisher of this book disclaim any liability, loss, or risk incurred as a direct or indirect consequence of the application of any content of this book. By reading and utilizing the content in this book, the reader agrees to be responsible for their own actions and decisions and to release the author and publisher from any liability.

CONTENTS

Introduction 1

Understanding the Concept of Zero-waste Kitchen 31

Steps to Transition into a Zero-waste Kitchen 60

Essential Tools for a Zero-waste Kitchen 91

Food Shopping for a Zero-waste Kitchen 121

Food Preparation in a Zero-waste Kitchen 151

Maintaining a Zero-waste Kitchen 181

Dealing with Waste in a Zero-waste Kitchen 212

Becoming Advocates for Zero-waste Living 242

Conclusion 272

INTRODUCTION

Acknowledgment and Gratitude

Appreciation for supportive family

The journey towards a 'Zero-waste Kitchen' begins with the acknowledgement of the problem, which is the tremendous waste that is currently generated in our kitchens. This book will not only provide insight into the implications of excessive waste on the environment but will also offer practical solutions that will help reduce its impact on our world. It will provide easy steps to follow in order to transform your kitchen from being a contributor to environmental problems to being a part of the solution.

This book is dedicated to all those who have always been keen on finding effective and sustainable ways of dealing with waste in our kitchens. It is for those who believe that transformation begins at home. To every discerning homemaker, dedicated chef, eco-conscious individual, and the forward-thinking generation, this book is for you.

Gratitude goes to my supportive family who has stood by me throughout this journey. They have been my cheering squad and my rock as I gathered information, tried various waste reduction techniques, and worked to put this manuscript together. They understood why I was so engaged and gave me useful opinions throughout the process. They tolerated my endless discussions about kitchen waste and helped with many of the experiments and attempts at creative waste management.

This book is also a product of many people's hard work and dedication. To the dedicated researchers, environmental activists, and eco-conscious individuals who have offered valuable insight and information to this project, thank you. Your work has helped shape the ideas in this book and the proposed guide to transform our kitchens.

The goal of the 'Zero-waste Kitchen' is not just to instill a sense of responsibility but to bring about a change in lifestyle, where sustainability and protection of the environment are at the forefront. We all have a role to play and a difference to make. Welcome to the journey of transforming your cooking space into an Eco-friendly haven.

Gratitude towards diligent research team

In the pursuit of a better and more sustainable world, many of us are making strides to transform various aspects of our daily lives. One important area that frequently is overlooked is the kitchen. Despite the fact that this space often forms the heart of our homes, we seldom give real consideration to the environmental impact that our cooking practices can have. It is towards resolving this disconnect that this book is directed.

The Zero-waste Kitchen, through its comprehensive outlook, seeks to transform your cooking space into an eco-friendly haven. The objective is simple. We wish to give you, the reader, the tools, the knowledge and the confidence to redefine your kitchen practices which are not just beneficial for the environment, but equally rewarding for you as well. Aiding in health benefits, reduced costs, and an overall improved quality of life, this transformation will reach well beyond your kitchen walls.

This literary pursuit would not have been possible without our diligent research team. They have dedicated countless hours examining a myriad of resources, to ensure that the information provided here is both practical and effective. Their substantial expertise, combined with their passion for environmental conservation, has proved invaluable.

We extend our sincerest gratitude to them, acknowledging the heart and effort they put into this project. They were, without a doubt, instrumental in this endeavor, ensuring that we could offer you the most accurate, up-to-date and easy-to-implement tips and techniques. Their commitment to the cause truly inspires us and I hope their work does the same for you.

As you delve into this book, you are not just reading a guide to eco-friendly kitchen practices, you are joining the tens of thousands of people determined to make a tangible impact on our environment. You are choosing a healthier and more ethical lifestyle. You are taking a step towards sustainability.

The journey towards a zero-waste kitchen may be less traveled, but it is one worth taking. As you flip the pages of this book and start to see your kitchen in a new, more conscious light, remember that every small step counts. And in this journey, you're never alone. We are with you in this quest for eco-friendly living, every step of the way.

We extend our warmest welcome to you, as you embark on this incredibly rewarding journey towards creating your own zero-waste kitchen. It is our sincere hope that these pages illuminate your path and foster in you the same passion for environmental conservation that motivated us to share this knowledge. Happy reading, and here's to creating kitchens that are not just the heart of our homes, but also guardians of our planet.

Acknowledgments to book editor

Yes, of course!

As dedicated professionals and aware citizens of the world, it's become apparent that a conscientious attitude towards our way of eating and preparing our food can greatly lessen the damage we inflict on the environment. The concept of "Zero-waste Kitchen" embodies that conscientious attitude, focusing not only on reducing waste but on creating a kitchen that is more sustainable and environmentally friendly.

An array of practiced techniques, seasoned ideologies, inspiring advice, and practical viewpoints have been collated together in this comprehensive guide. It serves as a valuable tool for those who are stepping onto the path of sustainable living for the first time as well as those who are well-versed in the movement. It is truly a comprehensive guide towards transforming your cooking space into an eco-friendly haven.

A book of this nature wouldn't have come into fruition without the collective effort and immense support of numerous individuals and entities. I wish to express my deepest gratitude to all those who have contributed towards the completion of this insightful guide.

I would like to extend a special thanks to my diligent book editor, whose expertise and dedication have greatly improved the scope and quality of this guide. Their unique perspective and sharp eye for detail have contributed significantly to the content and structure of this book. Through the process of their meticulous effort, the book has not only been enriched with valuable information but has also evolved into a very readable, engaging, and authoritative guide.

Overall, "The Zero-waste Kitchen" is much more than a book, it's an invitation to join a movement that fosters a healthier planet and nurturing home. It's a comprehensive guide that demands reflection, learning, and action. I do hope that this book will illuminate your path in your journey towards a more sustainable life. Your kitchen becomes the first step. And remember, every small step leads to a large screening positive effect.

Praise for sustainable living advocates

Most of us are familiar with the phrase, 'you are what you eat'. But in today's world dominated by one-time-use plastics, this statement gains another layer of inception: 'you are where you eat'. Indeed, our kitchen spaces, from which emanate the delightful scents of our daily sustenance, also become the origin of mammoth waste that invariably takes a toll on the environment. This book, 'The Zero-waste Kitchen: A Comprehensive Guide to Transforming Your Cooking Space into an Eco-friendly Haven', provides practical and easily achievable tactics to transform this highly functional space in our homes into an oasis of sustainability.

Before we delve deeper into the subject, I'd like to express my gratitude to everyone who supported me in this journey of gathering insights and knowledge to bring this guide to life. My heart is filled with profound appreciation for dedicated environmentalists, sustainability influencers, and green lifestyle advocates, whom I've had the pleasurable opportunity to interact with throughout the creation of this book. Their valuable input has contributed to enriching the content of 'The Zero-waste Kitchen' and making it perfect for anyone wanting to reduce their kitchen's environmental footprint.

Sustainable living isn't an overnight change; rather, it's a progression, a transformation that takes time to adapt and commit. Within the pages of this book, I applaud and celebrate everyone committed to this cause, their innovative solutions and their relentless efforts to advocate for a more sustainable lifestyle. Their work serves as an illuminating beacon for those seeking guidance in this field. They've shown us that it isn't about perfection but about making better choices each day and being consistently conscious of our impact on the environment.

As we progress through this guide, we'll learn to view our

kitchen spaces not just as a place to prepare meals, but as a key player in the larger ecosystem around us. We'll explore waste management, composting, growing our own produce, making the most out of food scraps, reducing plastic usage, sustainable shopping, and more. With mindful steps and an open mind, we can turn our kitchens into eco-friendly paradises, making it not only nourishing for us but for the planet as well.

Whether you are just beginning your journey towards a zero-waste kitchen or have long been an advocate of sustainable living, this guide promises to provide helpful tips and insights. It is my sincere hope that 'The Zero-waste Kitchen' serves as your faithful companion in your journey towards a greener, more sustainable lifestyle.

Thanks to dedicated readers

Welcome to your journey of transformation towards a lifestyle that is kind to both the environment and your wallet. 'The Zero-waste Kitchen' serves as your reliable guide to reimagining the way you cook, consume and dispose in your kitchen space, leading you gently towards achieving the goal of zero-waste.

Respecting our planet's limited resources has become a pressing issue in our modern lives. Therefore, directed by the values of sustainability and mindfulness, this book will show you how to transform your everyday actions in the kitchen into sustainable habits. From reducing food waste, to rethinking packaging, to introducing eco-friendly alternatives, each step in this journey helps to lighten our environmental footprint and make our kitchens a more harmonious space.

This journey into creating a zero-waste kitchen is not one of restriction or hardship, rather, it is an invitation to become more attentive to the ways in which we interact with our environment on a daily basis. It encourages creativity, frugality, and an awareness to make conscious choices that contribute to the long-term wellbeing of our planet.

Writing this all-encompassing guide would not have been feasible without the passionate individuals and dedicated organizations working tirelessly to safeguard our environment. Their unwavering dedication fuels the ongoing conversation around sustainability.

Also, this journey would be nonexistent without you, the readers, who have taken an active interest in transforming your lifestyle. Thank you for your endeavor to make a difference, for embracing change, and for creating a ripple effect that inspires those around you to live more sustainably.

In addition, I want to express my gratitude towards everyone who has shaped this book in one way or another. From the seed of its creation to its blossoming completion - your contributions, feedback, and relentless support have been invaluable.

In a world where we often feel disconnected from nature, this book serves as a practical aid and source of inspiration to reconnect with the natural world through the medium of our kitchens. Enjoy the journey to creating a thriving, eco-friendly haven in your home. Let the exploration begin.

A Sneak Peek into the Book

The kitchen waste conundrum

It is an undeniable truth that our kitchens are often the heart of our homes, and yet, they are also notorious for being the primary contributors to household waste. Excess packaging, food scraps, unused ingredients, and non-recyclable items often find their way into our garbage bins and subsequently, into our environment, causing unnecessary harm. This book, 'The Zero-waste Kitchen', aims to challenge our conventional perspective on kitchen waste and steer us towards transforming our cooking spaces into eco-friendly havens.

To address the escalating problem of kitchen waste, we first need to recognize the problem and understand its implications. Through this guide, we are embarking on a meaningful journey to identify the key waste categories, understand their environmental impacts, and most importantly, explore an array of sustainable alternatives to reinvent our practices in the heart of our homes – our kitchens.

This book presents a comprehensive roadmap to a zero-waste kitchen, offering practical, accessible and innovative strategies encompassing all aspects of a kitchen set-up, from cooking and cleaning to storage and dining. It will guide you through the process of adopting a zero-waste mindset, which extends well beyond merely reducing trash production. You will learn about the efficient utilization of resources and minimizing food waste, which are key components in the global endeavor to safeguard our planet for future generations.

Rest assured, 'The Zero-waste Kitchen' is not about impractical and hard-to-achieve goals. Rather, it is a journey of incremental changes, where each step, no matter how small, contributes to a larger aim of sustainable living. This guide will arm you with necessary tools and knowledge to make informed decisions about how you cook, clean, shop, and consume in your kitchen.

Expect engaging content that balances environmental science, gastronomy, and practical day-to-day tips to nurture and evolve into an eco-friendly household. This book will serve as a connector, blending eco-consciousness with your culinary endeavors, supporting you to make choices that not only nurture your family and community but also our Earth.

So, whether your current motive is to reduce your expenditure, declutter your spaces, lead a healthier lifestyle, or you are joining the fight against climate change, your path towards a waste-less kitchen starts here. This guide is a steppingstone to revamp your kitchen habits, your lifestyle choices, and ultimately, your impact on the world.

Envisioning the zero-waste kitchen

Conscious of the escalating environmental crisis and ever-expanding landfills, one might begin to reflect on their personal accountability. Our kitchen – the heart of our homes – becomes the starting point for this transformative journey. 'The Zero-waste Kitchen: A Comprehensive Guide to Transforming Your Cooking Space into an Eco-friendly Haven', meticulously unravels the mysterious, seemingly daunting, yet profoundly rewarding world that lies in creating a sustainable kitchen.

This book is not just about reducing kitchen waste; it represents a comprehensive exploration of a lifestyle shift that is both essential and urgent. It is designed to empower you, equipping you with the knowledge and practical know-how to transition into a zero-waste kitchen successfully.

Inside, we deeply delve into our habits, practices, and preferences surrounding cooking, shopping, and waste management, which are presently contributing to the rapidly degrading health of our planet. We understand that change can be challenging, and so, we take a sensitive, step-by-step approach to effectively alter our behavior.

Using eco-friendly alternatives, wise shopping habits, and creative waste management techniques, we illustrate how an attainable, cost-saving, and healthier kitchen environment can be achieved. We emphasize the importance of every kitchen activity, from selecting raw produce to the cleaning detergents used, demonstrating their impact on our personal health and the environment.

This book aims to foster understanding that a zero-waste kitchen isn't about perfection—it doesn't imply a radical, overnight change. Instead, it encourages gradual, mindful steps towards more sustainable choices, thus leaving a lesser environmental footprint. As you progress, you will find that these steps begin to naturally resonate with your values and daily routine—thus leading to more profound, long-term changes.

Fundamentally, this book hopes to impart that it's not solely about having a greener conscious. It's about taking ownership and responsibility for our actions, providing more than just a clean countertop but a safe, healthy, and sustainable living space. Moreover, it is about understanding that every decision we make in our kitchen can be a valuable contribution to a healthier planet—thereby making every meal an act of awareness and care.

In essence, 'The Zero-waste Kitchen' serves as an empowering guide to reimagining your relationship with food, the environment, and, ultimately, yourself. In the face of alarming environmental degradation, it's time we reassess and reconstruct our habits, adopting a lifestyle that rewards both us and the planet.

Understanding kitchen sustainability

For decades, the kitchen has been the heart of the home. It's where meals are cooked, occasions are celebrated, and family memories are made. But beyond the sentimental value, the kitchen can also be a hotspot for unnecessary waste. We've all been guilty of throwing away excess food or utilizing disposable items for the sake of convenience. However, with rising environmental concerns, the need to transition towards sustainability has never been greater.

Within the pages of this book, we venture into the concept of the zero-waste kitchen, exploring innovative ways to reduce waste, recycle materials and foster an environmental consciousness that transcends beyond your cooking space. It's not just about creating a kitchen that generates zero-waste but also about fostering a mindset that is conscious of every item's lifecycle, from procurement to disposal.

To begin, we delve into understanding the concept of kitchen sustainability and how it aligns with our daily practices. We'll explore the implications of our kitchen habits at both a macro level - affecting our environment, and a micro level - impacting our health and well-being.

The Zero-waste Kitchen offers a plethora of practical tips, easy-to-implement strategies, and intricate insights into how a sustainable kitchen can become a reality. It's an invitation to transform your cooking space from a waste generator to an eco-friendly haven. The entire process requires no significant overhaul but simply an attitude shift, a genuine understanding of the implications of waste, and steps to counter that.

It is about trainings, tools, techniques and remodeling – yes. But at heart it is about unseen things: about acquiring a new lens to look at our daily life and habits, about instilling a mindset that cares not only for the food that fills up bellies, but for the world that houses us.

Whether you're a novice starting on your journey towards sustainability, or you're well on your way and are searching for more eco-friendly ways to refine your habits, this book caters to readers from all walks of life.

This is an undertaking that promises not only environmental benefits but also rewards of an economic and health-oriented nature. As you move along this journey of transformation, feel the satisfaction and peace that stems from knowing that every small step taken contributes towards bigger, global shifts. Endeavor to adopt these strategic guidelines and watch how the ripples of your efforts touch not only your home but the entire ecosystem as well.

In essence, this book doesn't aim to dictate, but rather empower, inspire, and stimulate you in creating an efficient and eco-friendly kitchen. It encourages you to participate in the sustainability movement and lessen your environmental impact while still retaining the pleasures of cooking and sharing meals.

Welcome, then, to your first stride towards actualizing an eco-friendly haven starting right where your home pulses energetically: your kitchen.

Impact of eco-friendly cooking

Every corner of our abode embodies a part of our soul, and the kitchen is no exception. It's where the food, our primary survival need, is created. Imagine the power it wields over our well-being and the well-being of our planet.

This book introduces a crucial yet often overlooked aspect of an eco-friendly lifestyle - 'The Zero-waste Kitchen.' We aim to reorient your perspective towards your cooking space. We're not just talking about producing less waste but reimagining your kitchen as an eco-friendly haven in a practical, economically viable way.

As I dive deep into this subject and guide you through the process, I want to conduct a comprehensive appraisal of your kitchen as it stands today. What waste do you produce, and how often? How do you dispose of it? How do you source your cooking ingredients, and where do your leftovers end up? These are just a few of the questions we shall scrutinize as we embark on this transformational journey.

The Zero-waste Kitchen concept is not a fad but a philosophy, a lifestyle choice that serves more than your immediate surrounding. It contributes to battling a much larger global crisis - the environmental crisis. Indulging in wasteful activities while cooking, whether it is through excessive use of water or through unnecessary use of energy, we unknowingly contribute to the degradation of our environment.

By adopting sustainable cooking practices, one can significantly reduce one's carbon footprint, decrease the excess demand on limited natural resources, and manage our food better – thus leading to lesser waste. This book will help you apply the ideology of sustainability in your daily kitchen chores, through easy practices and practical solutions. Each one of us can step up and make a difference, starting within our home.

An eco-friendly kitchen might not seem a matter of pressing concern considering the magnitude of environmental issues we face. Still, it is through these seemingly small steps that we will collectively contribute towards a healthier and more sustainable planet.

So, prepare yourself to delve into the interconnections of your kitchen with the ecological network. You're about to be equipped with the wisdom of being a mindful inhabitant of this planet who understands the importance of sustainable living, right from the heart of your home - your kitchen.

Here's to the myriad ways in which we can, and we will transform our lives, aligning ourselves more closely with nature's rhythm - starting, of course, from the Zero-waste Kitchen. Welcome aboard on this transformational journey towards a sustainable lifestyle.

Journey of transformation

As we forge ahead into the 21st century, our kitchens, once the heart of our homes, have become catalysts for environmental harm. An alarming quantity of waste emanates from our cooking spaces: unused food, plastic packaging, disposable utensils, and energy wastage. However, with the escalating ecological crisis, it is more important than ever to transition toward more sustainable practices, to transform our kitchens into eco-friendly sanctuaries - where taste and sustainability are not combatants but harmonious allies.

This book, 'The Zero-waste Kitchen,' endeavors to guide you through this transformation. It is an actionable roadmap towards attaining a greener, cleaner, and ultimately more rewarding cooking space - one which is as pleasing for the palate as it is for the planet.

This journey will not happen overnight - it is, after all, a process of transformation. It invites you to make replacements, adopt healthy habits, and devise strategies that not only reduce waste but also incorporate ethical and sustainable practices right from procurement to disposal. Essentially, it aims to create a circular kitchen environment wherein waste is viewed not as trash that must be simply discarded, but as a valuable resource that could be reintegrated back into the kitchen system.

At first glance, the prospect of a 'Zero-waste Kitchen' might appear arduous. However, this transformation is fundamentally about small, manageable changes compounded over time. Through this book, you will learn that conservation does not necessarily mean compromise. In fact, these changes often lead to fresher, healthier, and more flavorful meals while reducing waste and saving money.

Embark on this transformative journey with an open mind

and a heart primed for change. Your efforts will reflect as a ripple effect, leading to a healthier home, a greener wallet, and ultimately, a more sustainable world. Remember, every small step is a leap towards larger environmental healing.

Welcome to a voyage of conservation and culinary delight - welcome to the era of the Zero-waste Kitchen.

Personal Notes

My journey to sustainability

In today's era of radical global climate changes and escalating environmental concerns, the concept of sustainability has never been more critical. It is present in every discussion pertaining to global growth and development. Yet, within this vast landscape of environmental solutions, I found my passion resting in one fundamental area of daily life - the kitchen.

My journey towards sustainability began like any other individual's - with a spark of curiosity and a smidgen of consciousness about the world we inhabit. However, what started as a simple curiosity soon evolved into a profound fascination and respect for the wondrous natural world. The more I discovered about the mounting environmental issues, the more I realized how our everyday actions contribute significantly to this global situation.

And like many of you, my daily routine revolved around the kitchen – a place not just for cooking, but also for nurturing relationships, indulging cravings, and exploring culinary adventures. But the kitchen was also a place that generated colossal amounts of waste daily, and that left an undeniable impact on me.

Taking the first steps towards transforming my kitchen into a zero-waste space was not an easy journey. There were moments of self-doubt, numerous failed experiments, and countless learning experiences. However, the more I plunged into this transformation, the more I realized the potential each of us holds in making a distinct and tangible impact on our planet through our kitchen practices.

In this book, you will find sachets of my journey, lessons learned, practical tips and tricks, and a comprehensive guide to help you manifest your own sustainable cooking space. My goal is to instill in you a sense of responsibility, awareness, and accessibility towards sustainable kitchen practices.

This transformation is not just about adopting environmentally friendly practices; it's about redefining our relationship with food, our kitchens, and ultimately with Mother Nature. I invite you to join me on this journey towards zero-waste, fostering respect for our environment, and revolutionizing our kitchen spaces into an eco-friendly haven.

A zero-waste kitchen

Entering the journey of sustainability can be an immense endeavor, especially for those who cook frequently or spend a substantial amount of time in the kitchen. It seems an impractical task, a utopian ideal far removed from reality. But, as a recipe transforms raw ingredients into a savory feast, I invite you to see the transformation of your cooking space into an ecological sanctuary that contributes to the preservation of our planet. This is the concept of a Zero-waste Kitchen, a paradigm shift made practically realizable in our daily lives.

'Zero-waste' isn't just a phrase or trend - it is a way of life that has the power to bring about meaningful change into our lives and our world. The kitchen, being the heart of our home, becomes the ideal starting point for such a transformation. By redefining the way we cook, eat and clean, we can nurture the seeds of sustainability and begin to bridge the gap between wellness and preservation. Our everyday food-related choices can move beyond our palates and stomachs and extend to the environment, impacting the amelioration or deterioration of our ecosystem.

Living with a Zero-waste mindset does not insist on perfection - far from it. Instead, it encourages an incremental transition towards sustainable practices that, when multiplied across communities, can pave the way towards significant global change. Reduction, reuse and recycling become more than just optional steps, transforming into a lifestyle pillar that benefits both your health and the planet.

Embracing a Zero-waste Kitchen challenges you to look beyond the conventional ideas of cooking and cleaning, to dig further into the choices of your ingredients, the kinds of cookware you use, and the ways in which you store your food. From reducing plastic to composting waste, each action embodies a valuable opportunity to make a difference.

Please step into this journey with an open mind and willingness to adapt. The implications of our alterations are extensive and significant. Keep in mind, the Zero-waste Kitchen venture is not accomplished overnight. Instead, it's a dedicated pursuit to be committed to every day, and every meal.

This guide will introduce you to the ideology behind the movements, provide tangible advice and actionable steps to transform your cooking practices, shopping behaviors, and provide space for reflection and growth. It is designed to nurture your growing understanding and provide practical assistance in your Zero-waste Kitchen journey.

It is my hope that as we explore these pages together, we'll not only change our kitchen, but we will also change our world, one meal at a time. Now, let's embark on this transformation together and embrace a greener, healthier kitchen lifestyle where waste is not an option, and sustainability is our shared goal. Welcome to your Zero-waste Kitchen.

Importance of eco-friendly practices

In today's contemporary world, the urgent need to implement eco-friendly practices in all facets of our lives has become increasingly evident. With the escalating ecological crisis, it is more important than ever to figure out how each one of us can contribute to a more sustainable future for our planet.

A substantial portion of the waste we generate originates from our homes, and particularly, our kitchens: food scraps, packaging, cleaning products, and much more. However, it is from this very place that we can initiate significant changes that would immensely contribute to the overall sustainability of our daily lives.

In establishing a zero-waste kitchen, we are not only minimizing our carbon footprint but are embarking on a journey towards a healthier lifestyle. The concept of zero-waste may seem daunting initially, replete with challenges. However, adopting this lifestyle doesn't necessarily entail drastic or instantaneous changes. Many people are under the misconception that pursuing a zero-waste environment is too complicated, expensive, or time-consuming. But if approached methodically and patiently, transitioning towards a zero-waste lifestyle can be a seamless, rewarding endeavor.

This guide aims to demystify the perception of the zero-waste lifestyle and unveil practical steps that can be taken to reduce waste produced in your kitchen. It is designed to educate and inspire, not only home cooks but anyone who aspires to make their cooking space more eco-friendly.

An eco-friendly kitchen doesn't simply reduce waste; it promotes a healthier lifestyle, instills clever and mindful habits, and is a testament to your commitment to environmental sustainability. With the right guidance and some effort, what may seem like a kitchen overhaul today could transform into an efficient and smooth-running green heaven for cooking.

The decision to adapt to an eco-friendly lifestyle is a personal one and subject to one's circumstances and commitment. Whether you're a seasoned environmentalist or a beginner in the realm of sustainability, there's something in this book for you. Keep in mind that it's not about perfection but progress, and every small step taken is a monumental stride towards achieving the overarching aim of sustainability.

In the following chapters, you will discover a variety of tips, tricks, and practices to set up and maintain your zero-waste kitchen. These will range from the basics like effective meal planning and smart shopping to more advanced techniques like composting and harnessing renewable energy for your cooking needs.

Welcome to a journey that is not only going to transform your kitchen space but also your relationship with food, waste, and the environment. As you begin, remember that the secret to successful implementation lies in taking one step at a time, embracing each small victory, and acknowledging that you are part of a broader global movement to safeguard our collective home - Earth.

Challenges in transition

The world today faces dire environmental challenges, unraveling at an alarming rate. Our dependency on ease and convenience, in tandem with ignorance and indifference, contribute to the decline of our planet's ecosystem. But we, as individuals, hold immense power in shaping the road to sustainability, starting with our very own kitchen.

'The Zero-waste Kitchen' aims to guide you on your journey towards an eco-friendly culinary environment. The goal is not perfection, but progress. It's not about immediate transformation, but the willingness to initiate change. This journey won't be easy. In fact, it might be challenging. This is where I come in as your guide and accomplice, using my experience as a coach and consultant to help navigate potential roadblocks in your path.

As we begin this journey, it's essential to discuss the challenges you may face while transitioning to a zero-waste kitchen. The transition can be testing due to an array of reasons - from new consumption habits, redefining convenience, unlearning and replacing deep-seated practices, to dealing with skeptical friends and family. Some challenges will be minor, easily overcome with a little change in attitude or practice. Others may take time, requiring patience, persistence, and continuous effort.

One key challenge arises from the disposable nature of today's societal practices. Single-use plastics and non-recyclable material are so deeply ingrained in our daily consumption, that it is daunting to consider a life without them. This switchover requires unlearning many of our daily habits and convenience, which can be difficult, both mentally and practically.

Secondly, you may also face resistance from those around you who struggle to understand or accept this lifestyle change. It's important to be patient, both with yourself and others, and remember that being proactive about educating oneself and others is a major part of this journey.

Being apprehensive about making changes is normal. However, overcoming these challenges will open up a model of life that is not only healthier and happier but also respects and treats the environment well. This book outlines various strategies, tips, and practical solutions to integrate zero-waste practices into your kitchen.

Remember, the transformation to a zero-waste kitchen does not lie solely in grand gestures, but in the small daily actions and decisions we make. Together, we can make your kitchen a sustainable sanctuary, one small step at a time.

Success story insights

The kitchen—a humble space often teeming with lively conversations, heart-warming meals, and occasionally, culinary disasters. Yet, beyond its traditional role, the kitchen offers a significant opportunity for eliciting positive environmental change. A standard kitchen can be a site of excessive waste, from food scraps to single-use packaging. Aware of this concern, many are now seeking practical strategies to transform their kitchens into eco-friendly havens. This book is a comprehensive guide designed to guide you through this transformation.

To create a zero-waste kitchen, it is not just about practical steps for waste reduction, but equally important, a change in perspective. In approaching this transition, it's useful to maintain the mindset that every small step, every bit of effort, matters. Progress doesn't require perfection. Mistakes, as they often are, will become our best teachers. In fact, my personal journey wasn't always smooth sailing. I met with stumbling blocks, lapses in judgement, and days filled with frustration. However, these moments spiraled into great learning opportunities, contributing to the strategies and insights you'll find in the pages to come.

This book will present the principles of a zero-waste kitchen—from understanding the waste pyramid to learning the art of preservation, planning meals efficiently, shopping with a zero-waste mentality, and recycling efficiently. I will share common scenarios that occur in the kitchen and provide solutions to handle them in an environmentally friendly way. Alongside this, anecdotes and success stories aim to inspire and reassure that change, though challenging, is not only achievable but also rewarding.

One such success story belongs to a family of four living in suburban Toronto. Initially inundated with their waste output, the Morgan family shared their holiday meals involving piles of discarded vegetable peels, endless plastic packaging, and a garbage can chock full of waste by the end of the day. Once they embraced the zero-waste kitchen approach, this scene dramatically changed. They started composting, preserving their leftovers, and initiated bulk buying using their own containers. Now, their trash can sit largely empty, while their compost bin teems with scraps soon to be returned to the earth. Their experience encapsulates the potential for profound transformations promised by a zero-waste kitchen.

We owe our commitment to our planet, our home. Reducing food waste and minimizing the use of non-recyclable items are more than just environmental activism—it's a lifestyle change that directly impacts our health, resources, and the future of our world. As you journey through this book, remember your mission and let it fuel your determination. With time, patience, and a persistent spirit, we can turn our kitchens—this intimate and essential part of our homes—into sustainable havens, contributing to a brighter, healthier planet.

UNDERSTANDING THE CONCEPT OF ZERO-WASTE KITCHEN

What is Zero-waste?

Definition of Zero-waste

Having an eco-friendly kitchen is no longer just an aspiration. It's a necessary move, not just for the health of the environment, but for the well-being of the inhabitants who use the kitchen space daily. A zero-waste kitchen is a significant component of this eco-friendly revolution. But what exactly does it entail?

The zero-waste concept is deeply ingrained in sustainable living practices. It's an ideology aimed at resource life cycle management, with the objective of reusing, recycling, and composting everything, hence sending nothing to landfills. The goal here is to make the most of each product and thus minimize the overall impact on the environment.

In the context of a kitchen, zero-waste means creating cooking spaces that are fully geared towards reducing waste. It embraces practices like buying in bulk, storing in reusable containers, composting kitchen scraps, and creatively using leftovers, all with a view to leaving a lighter footprint on our planet.

A zero-waste kitchen, therefore, it's not about perfection but progression. It involves moving from our conventional kitchen practices that generate a lot of waste towards more sustainable methods. These include measures such as reducing the use of plastic, choosing products with minimal packaging, using recyclable or compostable items, and composting organic waste.

The transition to a zero-waste kitchen requires intentionality, consciousness about consumption, and a commitment to change. Do not get overwhelmed by the enormity of the task. Perfecting a zero-waste kitchen practice is a journey that, when taken one step at a time, will inculcate habits that ultimately contribute to a sustainable future.

As we explore this guide, you'll learn that this transformation does not require massive overhauls or significant investment. Instead, it involves making minor adjustments to your daily routines, shopping habits, and food choices. The objective is to simplify the system, achieve efficiency, all while reducing the waste that ends up in the environment.

Your kitchen is a significant part of your life, and it can be a powerful tool in promoting earth-friendly practices. By choosing to operate a zero-waste kitchen, you're making a significant contribution to the health of our planet. With determination and small daily changes, you can take an essential and proactive step towards sustainability and eco-friendliness, starting right from your kitchen. A zero-waste kitchen is practical, achievable, and rewarding to both the environment and the kitchen users.

Origins of Zero-waste

The concept of a Zero-waste Kitchen revolves around the fundamental idea of reducing and eventually eliminating the disposal of waste materials into the environment. It champions practices that align with ideals of conserving and recycling to help not only maintain a sustainable kitchen space but also contribute towards a healthier environment.

'Zero-waste' is a philosophy that encourages the redesign of resource life cycles so that all products can be reused, thereby completely cutting off any garbage sent to landfills, incinerators, or even the ocean. The goal is to extract the maximum practical benefits from products while causing minimal harm to the environment.

This term extends beyond recycling because it emphasizes reducing and reusing first and recycling as a last resort. The primary intention is to prevent waste from being created in the first place, focusing on sustainable methods of waste management from the onset.

The origins of the Zero-waste concept traces back to the mid-20th century, where its roots were planted on the basis of concerns around resource extraction and consumption. However, it truly started gaining momentum in the late 1980s. Gary Liss, known as one of the pioneers in the zero-waste movement, played a significant role in the mainstreaming of this concept.

In the context of the kitchen, a Zero-waste approach would entail practices like composting food scraps, switching to reusable alternatives, buying in bulk to avoid unnecessary packaging, and so forth. By configuring our kitchen habits in this direction, we not only contribute to a sustainable environment but also adopt a healthier lifestyle by prioritizing fresh, natural, and non-processed ingredients.

Significance of Zero-waste

The concept of a Zero-waste Kitchen is a paradigm-shifting approach to how we prepare, consume, and dispose of our food. It is an ecological lifestyle shift dedicated to achieving a circular economy in the domain of your home kitchen, where no waste is produced, and entirely sustainable strategies are deployed. It embodies the principles of minimizing waste, aiming to send nearly nothing to landfills, incinerators, or the ocean. This holistic notion doesn't just imply the reduction of waste but its complete elimination.

So, what exactly does "Zero-waste" imply? At its core, zero-waste emphasizes the consistent reduction of materials that are considered waste to an absolute minimum. It epitomizes sustainable living, fostering the idea that everything we need to thrive can, and should, be sustainable, recyclable or compostable.

The quintessence of Zero-waste isn't just about waste diversion, it addresses the fundamental structure of a linear economy and works towards creating a circular one. It aims to halt the "'take, make, waste" cycle by considering the entire lifecycle of a product, from its creation to its disposition, and everything it interacts with throughout.

It's important to understand that a 'Zero-waste Kitchen' doesn't mean a complete extraction of packaging or a lifestyle overhaul overnight. It's about making effortful strides towards a sustainable lifestyle, keeping in mind the limitations and restrictions of your individual circumstances.

The significance of transitioning to a Zero-waste Kitchen is twofold. First, it significantly reduces the environmental footprint caused by kitchens. The kitchen is notoriously one of the highest waste-producing areas in homes, with food waste, plastic, and other non-sustainable materials at the forefront.

By transforming your kitchen into a zero-waste haven, you are making a direct and effective contribution to environmental preservation.

Second, going Zero-waste in the kitchen also has personal benefits. Consuming whole, non-packaged food is generally healthier, and the act of reducing waste is likely to prompt more mindful consumption and lifestyle habits. Moreover, it can also lead to substantial cost savings in the long term. Waste reduction means purchasing fewer items, reusing wherever possible, and thus only spending on necessaries.

In a world that's increasingly aware of its environmental impact, transitioning to a Zero-waste Kitchen isn't merely beneficial—it's vital. It ushers in a lifestyle that reveres sustainability, and actively contributes to a less polluted, healthier planet.

Implementation in Kitchen

The concept of a 'Zero-waste Kitchen' is rooted in the principle and philosophy of generating as little waste as possible. It presents a comprehensive approach to sustainability, an opportunity to evaluate our consumer habits, and rethink our approaches to food usage, storage, and disposal. The Zero-waste Kitchen approach is not only an environmental agenda but also a significant lifestyle shift that can contribute towards healthier living, mindful consumption, and economic savings.

'Zero-waste,' in its most literal sense, entails producing no waste at all, which could go to the landfill. Its goal is to ensure that all products are reused, and none burnt or dumped into the environment. It's centered around five key principles known as the 5 R's: Refuse, Reduce, Reuse, Recycle, and Rot. These principles highlight the steps that can guide us in limiting our ecological footprint, aiming to design out waste and pollution, keep items and materials in use, and regenerate natural systems.

In the context of the kitchen, 'Zero-waste' demands scrutiny of our food planning, shopping, storage, cooking, and discarding habits. Paradoxically, the kitchen, which is the heart of our homes and comfort spaces, could potentially contribute to a substantial part of household waste, given the frequency of cooking, the volume of food waste generated, and the packaging that most food items come in.

Implementing a Zero-waste Kitchen is a journey. While it may seem daunting at first, it's crucial to realize that small, incremental changes can bring about substantial differences. It starts with a shift in perspective - viewing waste as a consequence of our decisions and habits. Essential steps such as planning meals in advance, buying only what is necessary, storing food properly, fully utilizing ingredients in cooking, recycling or composting kitchen scraps, and favoring reusable containers, can considerably mitigate waste.

Packaging plays a massive role in a Zero-waste Kitchen strategy. Bulk shopping helps to significantly reduce single-use plastic packaging. Encouraging the use of reusable shopping bags, glass or metal containers and saying no to plastic cutlery and straws are all viable strategies.

The Zero-waste Kitchen synergizes environmental consciousness and practicality in a functionally aesthetic space that can simultaneously encourage healthier living and responsible consumption. The point is to adopt and adapt, to experiment, and to learn, while simultaneously striving to treat our environment with the respect it deserves.

Benefits and Challenges

In this era of environmental concerns, having a zero-waste kitchen has never been more critical. Embracing a zero-waste lifestyle, led by one's kitchen, serves as a practical and efficient approach to environmental sustainability. A zero-waste kitchen is exactly what it sounds like – a cooking space that functions with the ambition of creating the least amount of waste possible.

At its core, the zero-waste movement aims to send nothing to landfills, incinerators, or the ocean. It's a novel practice based on the principle of rethinking how to use resources to minimize, if not outright eradicate, the amount of waste produced. This concept calls for a lifestyle shift, replacing the linear 'take, make, dispose' model of resource handling with a closed-loop system. This circular approach promotes the 5 R's - Refuse, Reduce, Reuse, Recycle, and Rot.

By adopting a zero-waste lifestyle in your kitchen, you not only contribute towards reducing environmental harm, but there are also benefits that directly impact you. Firstly, it leads to healthier living choices as it encourages a diet rich in real, unprocessed foods. Notably, it also leads to profound cost savings in the long run by fostering intentional practices of food preparation, consumption, and storage. Moreover, a zero-waste kitchen attributes to reduced clutter and promotes an efficient, well-organized kitchen space.

However, transitioning to a zero-waste kitchen does have its challenges, especially at the outset. Old habits can be hard to break, and the initial setup of a zero-waste can require a substantial time investment until new routines are ingrained. The pervasive reliance on disposables and the lack of zero-waste alternatives in conventional food supply chains can also be stumbling blocks. Furthermore, living a zero-waste lifestyle often calls for a conscious commitment to consistent effort, vigilance, and learning.

Nonetheless, these challenges should not deter you from endeavoring towards a zero-waste kitchen. The road to zero-waste is less about perfection and more about making better choices gradually and consistently. The transition can start with simple steps. With an informed understanding of effective techniques, product alternatives, and mindful practices, you can transform your kitchen into an eco-friendly haven, one step at a time. Above all, remember that every small change counts in the grand scheme of reducing waste, conserving resources, and preserving the environment for future generations.

How it Relates to Your Kitchen

An eco-friendly lifestyle transformation

Like unraveling yarn from a knit sweater, understanding the concept of a Zero-waste Kitchen involves tracing back the intricate webs of waste creation in one's everyday life - beginning foremost in our kitchen. The kitchen, as a culinary playground and a central hub for most activities in homes, generates a significant amount of waste. This may range from food disposals to non-recyclable packaging, single-use cutlery, and a series of other seemingly trivial, but immensely damaging, waste items.

Transforming your cooking space into a Zero-waste Kitchen denotes not merely an aesthetic alteration, but a profound shift in your lifestyle, relationships, and interactions with the environment. The Zero-waste Kitchen requires a commitment to reducing, reusing, recycling, repairing, and refusing as key principles of sustainability. These principles woven into your daily habits enable a radical reduction in waste generation, ultimately tangibly impacting the ecosystems in which we dwell.

But what does this transformation mean for your kitchen?

To begin, the Zero-waste Kitchen is not a utopian, unreachable ideal. Instead, it is an attainable reality, grounded in mindful practices and informed consumption decisions that reshape your cooking space into an eco-friendly haven. It implies a shift from disposable and non-sustainable goods to reusable, compostable, or recyclable items. It means choosing metal or bamboo straws over their plastic counterparts, cloth napkins over paper ones, and glass jars instead of plastic containers.

However, the transformation transcends beyond these physical aspects, reaching the food that you consume. A

Zero-waste Kitchen fosters a deeper connection with your food, its producers, and its journey from the farm to your fork, encouraging local, seasonal, and organic eating, while harnessing a stronger commitment to food's end-life cycle through composting.

In essence, the Zero-waste Kitchen transforms the mundanity of everyday chores into an enriching and educative journey that builds an authentic connection with the environment and fosters a truly sustainable lifestyle. This transformation fuels a deeper understanding of the intricate and often invisible relation between our daily practices and their broader ramifications on social and environmental structures, crafting a kitchen space that serves not only us but the world that hosts us.

Minimizing food waste

The Zero-waste Kitchen offers a distinct and timely approach towards modern culinary practices, promoting environmental sustainability through the strategic reduction and eventual elimination of waste. It advocates for the creation of a cooking space that thrives on efficient practices and responsible disposal, paying homage to the paradigm of a circular economy.

Zero-waste as a term refers to the significant minimization and ideally, the total elimination of waste. Adapted to the kitchen setting, it implies the careful use of raw materials, wise food preparation, smart storage, and the effective use of leftovers, all aimed at reducing the amount of waste that comes out of our kitchens.

The principle of a zero-waste kitchen is a response to the ongoing global environmental crisis influenced in part by domestic activities, such as cooking which often results in unnecessary waste. Food leftovers, unused ingredients, single-use packaging, all these contribute to the waste that clogs our landfills, pollutes our waters, and affects our air quality. A zero-waste kitchen counters this wastefulness and promotes an eco-friendly, mindful lifestyle.

The relevance of a Zero-waste Kitchen to your domestic routine cannot be overstated. Apart from creating an environmentally conscious kitchen, adopting such practices allows for efficient usage of resources, leading to less food waste and more monetary savings. Embracing this concept can incite a significant decrease in the amount of garbage that each household produces daily, directly influencing the health and sustainability of our shared environment.

Reducing food waste starts with meticulous meal planning

and smart grocery shopping. Choose fresh items that you will use up in the next few days and buy grains, legumes, and dry goods in bulk to reduce packaging waste.

Learn more about proper food storage to extend the life of your fresh goods. Invest in airtight containers, consider freezing surplus fruits and veggies or learn quick pickle recipes to preserve them longer. Scraps and peels from raw produce can be composted, providing excellent nutrition for home-grown herbs or other container plants.

Lastly, learn to consider leftovers not as waste, but as components for future meals. Plan meals that can easily be remodeled into new meals - a roasted chicken one night can become chicken salad for lunch the next day or simmer the bones for a nutritious broth. By viewing all food as valuable, you'll begin to inherently minimize waste.

The transition towards a zero-waste kitchen may seem challenging. However, it is a worthy endeavor that yields bountiful benefits - not only for individual households but on a larger scale, for our planet. Remember, every small action to mitigate waste contributes to a more sustainable world. Let your kitchen be the start of that change.

Utilizing resources efficiently

An ecological awakening is undoubtedly taking place in our global society, with more and more individuals, corporations, and governments seeking ways to lessen their environmental impact and promote sustainable practices. One particular area where this movement is making significant strides is in the kitchen, where the adoption of a zero-waste approach can have a profound effect on our carbon footprint and overall wellbeing.

The zero-waste kitchen isn't merely about recycling or composting. It is a paradigm shift, a fundamental change in how we perceive and treat our food and the infrastructural components of our culinary space. It involves reimagining traditional recipes, rethinking food storage, and fostering innovative ways to reduce, reuse, and recycle.

To truly comprehend the notion of a zero-waste kitchen, picture a cooking domain that utilizes resources with such prudence and precision that waste is virtually non-existent. This involves a meticulous approach to meal planning, careful selection of food items, deliberate storage methods aimed to extend the lifespan of foodstuffs, and the categorization of leftovers as ingredients for future meals instead of waste.

The concept of a zero-waste kitchen is not intended to be intimidating nor inaccessible. Rather, it is a practical methodology that, once understood and applied, can be surprisingly simple and incredibly gratifying. It starts with changing your mindset about what constitutes waste and recognizing that almost everything has utility if utilized thoughtfully and resourcefully.

Your own kitchen is a universe teeming with opportunities for a more sustainable lifestyle, waiting for you to tap into its potential. Every component in it, your appliances, pots, pans, food stock - all provide you with numerous chances for efficiently using resources. From reusing freezer bags, composting vegetable trimmings, to approaching food shopping with a view to minimizing packaging, every choice made can bring you closer to operating a zero-waste kitchen.

In conclusion, the journey to having a zero-waste kitchen is not one marked by perfection but constant effort and improvement. It is a forward-thinking endeavor that greatly contributes to the environmental health of our planet, and the wellbeing of our homes. The key to this revolution lies in conscious decisions, thoughtful purchases, innovative repurposing, and mindful consumption. In transforming your kitchen into an eco-friendly haven, you will be making notable strides towards a healthier planet and a healthier you.

Sustainable kitchen practices

The world is gripped with numerous challenges, with environmental conservation taking a prime spot. The kitchen, being a focal point of daily human interaction, presents vast opportunities to contribute significantly towards the betterment of our environment. By adopting the zero-waste kitchen concept, we can reduce our carbon footprint and make our cooking space a nurturing hub for sustainable practices.

The zero-waste kitchen concept is twofold. Firstly, it focuses on reducing waste generated in our kitchens, from food scraps to packaging materials. Secondly, it emphasizes the repurposing and recycling of waste, only when it's impossible to avoid. This approach inclines towards a circular economy, where we focus on maximizing the utility of every item to its longest potential lifespan, before considering disposal.

Understanding this concept is one thing; how does it translate to your kitchen? It begins with a consciousness of how we can make everyday activities in our kitchen greener and eco-friendly. It may start with reducing waste generated from food, by cleverly planning meals ahead to avoid grocery surplus, learning how to properly store food to last longer, and transforming leftovers into delectable meals.

One sustainable kitchen practice that aligns perfectly with this concept is composting. Instead of throwing out vegetable peels, coffee grounds or eggshells, consider composting them. This creates nutrient-rich soil that can be used for growing plants. Moreover, utilizing compost bins can help to decrease the amount of biodegradable waste that ends up in landfills, thereby reducing overall greenhouse gas emissions.

Moreover, purchasing in bulk or opting for groceries with less packaging are ways to cut down plastic waste. Also, choosing reusable items over single-use options contributes to your creation of a zero-waste kitchen. For example, using cloth towels in place of paper ones, and glass containers instead of plastic bags makes your kitchen more sustainable.

Lastly, recycling should be the last resort if waste creation is unavoidable. As we know, not all items are compostable or reusable and thus, segregating waste for recycling plays a vital role in our endeavor towards a zero-waste kitchen.

It is important to remember that deploying the zero-waste kitchen concept is not just about taking on new practices. It's equally about unlearning some ingrained habits. While transitioning can seem tedious initially, the ensuing fulfillment far outweighs the early inconvenience. The journey to shaping your kitchen into an eco-friendly haven is progressive, one that redefines our relationship with the environment while placing our kitchens at the forefront of sustainability.

Homemade natural cleaners

Understanding the concept of a zero-waste kitchen begins with the realization of the interrelatedness between our domestic habits and the wider environmental concerns. It's alarming to think about how our daily kitchen activities such as cooking, cleaning, storing food, and even discarding waste can contribute to environmental issues like pollution, deforestation, and global warming. By embracing the zero-waste kitchen philosophy, we start a ripple effect of positive changes in our households leading to a more sustainable planet.

The zero-waste kitchen, at its core, revolves around creating the least possible amount of waste while maximizing the use of resources within our cooking spaces. It necessitates a transformation that goes beyond reusing, recycling, or reducing; it requires a lifestyle change that instils responsibility, creativity, and a conscious decision to tread lightly on our Earth.

The relation of this concept to your kitchen is direct and significant. Kitchens are the heart and hub of our homes - they symbolize sustenance, nurturing, and gathering. They are also probably the place where most household waste is generated. Given its pivotal role, transforming your kitchen into an eco-friendly haven goes a long way in contributing to environmental preservation. It involves more thoughtful meal planning, smarter shopping habits, innovative storage solutions, and more considerate ways of disposing of kitchen waste.

One practical step in the right direction is embracing homemade natural cleaners. Traditional cleaning products are often laden with harsh chemicals that not only harm the environment but can also jeopardize our health. On the other hand, homemade natural cleaners, made from simple and readily available ingredients like vinegar, baking soda, and lemons, provide a safer and healthier alternative. These alternatives are not only beneficial to the environment and us, but they are also cost-effective. Plus, the process of making natural cleaners is surprisingly easy and empowering - nothing quite compares to whipping up your concoction that cleans effectively without leaving a negative footprint.

In essence, cultivating a zero-waste kitchen is a revolutionary step towards greater sustainability. It allows us to rethink our habits, question our consuming patterns, and rediscover the magic of creating more with less. It reminds us that in every meal we prepare, every container we reuse, and every chemical-free cleaner we whip up, we are making a positive impact on our planet. Our kitchen becomes more than just a cooking space - it becomes a beacon of our commitment to love and protect the Earth.

Impact of a Zero-waste Kitchen

Reduces environmental harm

The concept behind a 'Zero-waste Kitchen' isn't just about minimizing physical waste; it extends into every facet of the cooking and consumption process, including water usage, energy efficiency, sourcing of materials, and responsible disposal techniques. Incorporating these paradigms into your daily routines can drastically reduce your environmental footprint and provide a profound sense of accomplishment and stewardship for the environment.

The impact of a Zero-waste Kitchen on the environment is significant and, more importantly, instantly visible. Globally, food waste contributes to approximately 8% of all greenhouse gas emissions. A Zero-waste Kitchen is a solution to this global problem. It means being conscious of our resources, making choices that are consistent with sustainability, and adopting practices that will not deplete or damage the environment.

Reducing harm to the environment means placing value on nature's resources and respecting the natural rhythms of the planet. It entails using reusable containers instead of single-use plastics, composting organic waste rather than letting it decompose in a landfill, purchasing in bulk to reduce packaging waste, and so much more. Moreover, a Zero-waste Kitchen focuses on conservation of energy and water through smart practices and appliances.

It's an approach that emphasizes the reduction of waste through practices such as recycling, composting, and careful consumption. Reducing waste not only shrinks your ecological footprint but also results in savings. It optimizes usage and eliminates surplus, thereby promoting efficiency on all fronts.

Adopting the tenets of a Zero-waste Kitchen isn't just about saving the environment. It's about transforming the way we think about waste, getting creative with what we might consider trash, and cultivating a sustainable mindset that permeates all aspects of life. A Zero-waste Kitchen is more than a notion – it's a lifestyle, an ethos, a statement of preserving the earth for future generations. It guides us towards an era of sustainable living, underlining the importance of balance between the consumption and conservation of natural resources.

In essence, the Zero-waste Kitchen is not only a paradigm shift in culinary habits; it's a profound societal change that forces us to reassess our relationship with the environment. By diligently pursuing this goal, we can ensure both the planet and its people thrive for generations to come.

Promotes sustainable living

Understanding the concept of a zero-waste kitchen requires contemplating your current relationship with waste, food, and the space where you transform raw ingredients into nourishment. It involves developing a deeper awareness of your food consumption patterns, cooking practices, and disposal habits, along with a commitment to modify these behaviors towards more sustainable alternatives.

The zero-waste kitchen is a paradigm shift from the conventional kitchen characterized by single-use items, plastic packaging, and excessive food waste. It encourages a transition to more conscious choices such as opting for bulk purchases, choosing unprocessed foods, maximizing leftovers, composting organic waste, and shifting from disposable to reusable kitchen tools. The main objective is to reduce or eliminate the output of waste from your kitchen as much as possible.

The impact of a zero-waste kitchen relays far beyond merely reducing physical waste. First, it positively influences the overall ecological footprint by cutting down on pollution linked to waste disposal, including landfills and incineration. There is also a significant reduction in the amount of plastic that ends up in our oceans, thereby protecting marine life.

Second, there are substantial economic benefits. Adopting a zero-waste kitchen approach can be cost-effective in the long run. It leads to smarter food purchases, decreases unnecessary spending on single-use items, and reduces the hidden costs associated with waste management.

Third, a zero-waste kitchen promotes healthier eating habits. By focusing on whole, unprocessed foods, you will be managing your health and simultaneously, reducing packaging waste.

Lastly, having a zero-waste kitchen can be deeply empowering. It fosters a sense of competence and ownership over one's environmental impact, which can permeate into other areas of one's life.

Consequently, a zero-waste kitchen significantly promotes sustainable living. Its principles align with the wider sustainability framework of reducing resource usage, reusing materials, recycling when reusing isn't possible, and always prioritizing respect for the environment. Implementing the strategies of a zero-waste kitchen can mark a powerful individual contribution to the global objective of a healthy, sustainable earth.

To conclude, understanding the zero-waste kitchen ethos and integrating it into your lifestyle can be immensely rewarding. It is not merely about creating an eco-friendly haven within your own home, but also about fostering a healthier environment, economy, and society. It emphasizes that every individual's actions, no matter how small they may seem, collectively have a profound impact on the well-being of our planet.

Prevents wastage of food

The concept of a zero-waste kitchen is a paradigm shift from the conventional, resource-intensive, and waste-generating mode of kitchen operation to a sustainable, efficient, and utterly waste-free cooking sanctuary. As the name suggests, a zero-waste kitchen aims for a drastic reduction in waste generation by focusing on practices that avoid waste from the onset. It's a philosophy that fosters keen consideration of every purchase, every use, and every disposal, underlining the importance of exhausting the lifecycle of each product and committing to recycling or composting when ultimate disposal becomes inevitable.

Underpinning this concept is the well-established waste hierarchy, known as the Three R's - Reduce, Reuse, and Recycle. The zero-waste kitchen takes this principle to heart, adding a fourth 'R' for 'Refuse', aiming to decline any product or practice that contributes to unnecessary waste. The ideology's ultimate goal is the total elimination of waste; however, it understands that this is a process requiring significant changes in behavior, habits, and lifestyle. Still, each small step towards producing zero-waste contributes to this bigger picture.

Pivoting to a zero-waste kitchen has a profound impact, both at the micro and macro level. Individually, it allows for the effective utilization of resources, encouraging mindful eating, and reducing household spending. By investing in reusable, durable goods, the need for disposable, single-use items is eliminated, thereby conserving resources and saving money in the long-term.

On a broader scale, the zero-waste kitchen impacts our environment significantly by lightening the load on landfills, conserving natural resources, and reducing pollution from waste treatment and disposal. Each act of prevention, be it composting organic waste, recycling materials, or opting for package-free groceries, contributes to the resilience of our ecosystems and the longevity of our planet.

Preventing food wastage is a central theme in a zero-waste kitchen. Approximately a third of all food produced globally for human consumption is wasted or lost - equivalent to 1.3 billion tons per year, according to the Food and Agricultural Organization of the United Nations. This wastage is not just a misuse of food itself but also of the resources employed in its production.

In a zero-waste kitchen, you prioritize planning meals, shopping mindfully, storing food effectively, and learning to use every part of the items you cook with, including those traditionally discarded. Creative cooking also comes into play, using leftovers or creating broths and compost with food scraps. This holistic approach to utilizing our food not only reduces waste but increases our appreciation of the nourishment we have at our disposal.

In essence, a zero-waste kitchen is not just an eco-friendly shift in our cooking space. It is an affirmation of our responsibility towards the planet and future generations. Each choice to reduce, refuse, reuse, and recycle brings us a step closer to sustainability, resilience, and a healthier world. By creating a zero-waste kitchen, we turn our cooking space into a conduit for environmental change, one meal at a time.

Encourages creative reusability

In the journey towards creating a sustainable lifestyle, understanding the concept of a Zero-waste Kitchen is a significant milestone. For many, the kitchen is the heart of the home, a place of creativity and nourishment. But it is also often a significant source of waste, from excess food that rots in the back of the fridge to disposable containers that are used once and then discarded. By striving to achieve a Zero-waste Kitchen, we can significantly reduce the environmental impact our domestic lives impose.

The Zero-waste Kitchen is not just a hypothetical concept; it is an approach of practical changes, reducing waste gradually yet consistently. It shifts the perspective from taking out multiple bags of garbage each week to striving to eliminate waste altogether. It urges us to conscientiously adopt sustainable habits, focusing on reducing, reusing, recycling, and composting to minimize the amount of waste that ends up in landfills.

The reality of plastic pollution and food waste is distressing. Plastics take hundreds of years to decompose, with a majority of it ending up in the ocean, causing havoc on sea life. Meanwhile, food waste creates significant amounts of methane - a potent greenhouse gas - when they decompose in landfills. Visualize the trash we produce as an ever-growing, tangible embodiment of these environmental issues. Creating a Zero-waste Kitchen aims to tackle this growing concern by cutting down on plastics and limiting food waste.

A Zero-waste Kitchen also encourages creative reusability, urging one to reconsider the life cycle of a product beyond its first use. Consider, for instance, glass jars that once held jams or pickles. Rather than tossing the empty containers into the recycling bin, these jars can be reused for storing bulk pantry items, making homemade jams or salad dressings, or even as rustic drinking glasses or vases. This approach goes beyond merely 'recycling,' placing emphasis on 'reusing' in the most innovative sense.

By transforming your cooking space into a Zero-waste Kitchen, you are contributing to the preservation of our environment, but also to the enhancement of your creativity and the improvement of your health. It invites a prudent mindset where every product has significant value, and nothing goes to waste. It challenges us to live more sustainably and encourages a lifestyle that is not only beneficial to us, but also to future generations.

In essence, a Zero-waste Kitchen is more than a conceptual figment. It's a lifestyle shift, focusing on creating a mindful, sustainable living space. It's a simple yet powerful way to become an everyday environmental superhero.

Decreases consumeristic tendencies

The concept of a Zero-waste Kitchen takes root in humanity's burgeoning commitment to conserving the environment. It manifests a conscious decision to reduce waste generation, reuse products where viable, and recycle or compost inevitable waste. It is based on the principles of responsible consumption.

A Zero-waste Kitchen indicates an innovative approach to the use and disposal of kitchen resources. It encourages a shift away from reliance on disposable goods, towards the embrace of reusable, sustainable, and biodegradable products. The emphasis is placed on reducing where possible and reusing or recycling what can't be prevented. In essence, it is about adjusting the mindset, switching to a circular economy approach instead of being stuck in the age-old linear 'take-make-waste' model.

Moving towards a Zero-waste Kitchen, and by extension a zero-waste lifestyle, requires going beyond managing waste that has already been generated, to preventing waste from being produced at all. It requires looking beyond just the economic impact of a product, to its environmental and socio-cultural impact as well.

The Zero-waste Kitchen fundamentally alters the dynamic between the consumer and the consumed. By encouraging conscious decision-making when it comes to consumption, it diminishes the propensity toward consumerism and fosters a sense of responsibility. An essential aspect of this transformative journey involves acknowledging the direct correlation between purchasing behaviors and the volume of waste generated.

By decreasing consumeristic tendencies, we also reduce the over-consumption of resources. Every product we buy has a life cycle. It's made, used, and disposed of. In a consumerist society, this process often results in product surplus and resource exhaustion which eventually leads to wastage.

A Zero-waste Kitchen, chiseled by conscious and intentional decisions concerning consumption, profoundly impacts the environment, economic health, and overall sustainability. It translates into reduced landfills, cleaner landscapes, and preserved natural resources. Thus, redefining our interaction with the kitchen twists the narrative from a mere cooking space to a crucible for environmental stewardship.

In conclusion, a Zero-waste Kitchen marks a significant shift in value systems, placing environmental sustainability at its core. It fuels a radical transformation where individual justice merges with environmental justice, where conscious consumerism fosters a future that caters for today's needs without compromising the ability of future generations to meet theirs.

STEPS TO TRANSITION INTO A ZERO-WASTE KITCHEN

Planning and Organization

Evaluate Kitchen Habits

Transitioning to a zero-waste kitchen requires a careful approach that involves planning, organization, and evaluation of your current kitchen habits. It's not a process that happens overnight, but with commitment and patience, you can make significant strides towards a sustainable lifestyle.

Step One: Evaluate Your Kitchen Habits

Your journey to a zero-waste kitchen starts with acknowledging and analyzing the waste you already produce. For about a week, observe closely how much trash you generate, identifying what it's composed of, and how it came about. Keeping a waste journal could help you track common items and see patterns. The goal here is to increase your awareness of your personal consumption and waste habits, recognition that will become crucial as you transition.

Step Two: Identify and Prioritize Changes

Having evaluated your kitchen habits, you will probably notice certain areas contributing more to waste. It could be excessive packaging from store-bought items, unused leftovers, reliance on single-use items, or something else specific to your household. Identify these areas and use them as your starting points.

It's not practical, nor is it recommended to implement all strategies at once. Prioritize changes that make the most impact and that you feel ready to undertake. Gradually introduce more steps over time. This way, it will be much easier to make sustainable changes without feeling overwhelmed.

Step Three: Planning and Organization

One of the key components of a zero-waste kitchen is the strategic planning and organization of your daily cooking habits and space. It includes reevaluating your grocery shopping habits, meal planning, and optimal use of kitchen storage.

Before heading to the grocery store, make a list of necessary items, checking your pantry to avoid duplicate buying. Rotate items so that the most perishable ones are used first. Plan meals ahead of time, considering how to use leftovers creatively, and try to buy only what's needed for planned meals.

Equally, kitchen storage plays a crucial role in reducing waste. Utilizing glass jars for bulk buying, and storage containers for regulating portion sizes can significantly limit the amount of waste we generate. The key here is to ensure that everything has a place, and that each item serves a particular purpose.

Step Four: Education and Experimentation

A significant portion of the journey to a zero-waste kitchen is education and experimentation. Learning new methods to repurpose or compost food scraps, understanding how to recycle properly, and generally exploring ways to be more efficient can be a fun experiment. At the same time, it's important to stay open to new strategies and ideas that can help you decrease waste further.

Remember that the goal of a zero-waste kitchen is not perfection, but progress. It's about implementing sustainable habits that align with your lifestyle, and sparking change that can lead to a more environmentally conscious society. Every action counts—no matter how small. It's a journey that will not only transform your kitchen but can also have a profound impact on your lifestyle and the environment as a whole.

Determine Waste Hotspots

Transitioning into a zero-waste kitchen involves adopting new habits and changing perspectives. It's not only about doing away with plastic but promoting a lifestyle that values resource efficiency, environmental preservation, and overall sustainability. This transformation, albeit a transformative one, should be rewarding and fulfilling for you and your family. Remember that perfection isn't the goal here but progress.

To create your personal zero-waste kitchen, thorough planning and organization will be crucial. This will help you establish a functional kitchen space that aligns with your sustainability goals.

The first step to proper planning lies in evaluating your current kitchen practices. Essentially, you need to determine where your waste is coming from. We call these areas 'waste hotspots'.

It could be your grocery shopping habits, where you end up buying more than needed leading to waste. Or perhaps, it's the lack of composting for food scraps that goes directly into the bin. It might also be related to convenience-packaged foods that generate great amounts of non-recyclable waste. Once you've identified these hotspots, you'll be better positioned to target and reduce problematic waste components.

The next step is to outline the changes you'll make to these practices. If over-purchasing is an issue, start by creating a meal plan and shopping list, buying only what you need for the week. If a lack of composting is causing waste, start researching the composting options that are feasible for you, whether it's vermicomposting or using a compost service. If packaged foods are the problem, consider making more meals from scratch and using whole foods that are often less packaged or can be bought in bulk.

Remember, the goal of a zero-waste kitchen is not necessarily to produce zero-waste, but rather to conserve resources and reduce the amount of waste that ends up in our landfills and oceans.

A zero-waste kitchen requires patience and consistency as it's a journey and not a destination. You're not going to be perfect at first, but that's alright. With time, you'll find that these practices become habits, and your kitchen will transform into a more sustainable, eco-friendly haven.

Let this be a transition that brings joy, not stress. Celebrate your progress and remember that every little action can be a powerful contribution to a more sustainable future. Above all, let your kitchen not just be a place for cooking, but also a platform for practicing environmental responsibility. Let it echo your commitment to nature, one meal at a time.

Planning Eco-friendly Meals

Initiating the transition into a Zero-waste Kitchen might seem daunting at first glance, but with thorough planning and organization, anyone can turn their cooking space into an ecological sanctuary. Integrating the principle of sustainability into your lifestyle, starting with the kitchen, opens the gateway to a healthier and more fulfilling way of living.

Begin by re-evaluating your current habits. Assess how much waste you generate on average and identify potential causes. Examine your shopping, cooking, and disposal practices. Track patterns that contribute to waste production and determine if they can be modified or replaced with sustainable alternatives.

Armed with these insights, proceed with decluttering your kitchen. Remove items that are rarely used and everything that contributes toward creating waste. Replace them with sustainable options such as glass containers, silicone bags, beeswax wraps, and other reusable and recyclable options. Reorganize your kitchen to make space for recycling, composting, and proper waste disposal systems. Pay attention to food storage locations too - proper food storage can considerably extend the life of ingredients, thereby reducing waste.

The next phase is refining your shopping strategy. Embrace the culture of bulk shopping, invest in reusable grocery bags, and buy unpacked fresh fruits, vegetables, and other items whenever possible. Choose local produce to support regional farmers while reducing carbon footprints associated with long transportation. Negate using plastic bags for weighable items; instead, opt for reusable mesh or fabric bags.

Proceed to plan your meals carefully. Align your meal plans to your grocery shopping frequency to reduce food wastage. For instance, plan perishable ingredients at the beginning of your meal cycle and reserve non-perishable or frozen foods for later in the week. Start a kitchen diary where you can jot down the patterns of your grocery consumption and adjust your buying and cooking habits accordingly.

When it comes to cooking, practice portion control. Only cook the amount you'll consume to avoid leftover waste. And even if there are leftovers, store them properly for the next meal or compost them if they're unfit for consumption.

Lastly, establish an eco-friendly waste management system. Composting food scraps not only helps in minimizing waste output but also enriches your garden soil. Recycle items responsibly and ensure the correct segregation of waste.

In conclusion, transforming your kitchen into a Zero-waste zone is a journey that demands commitment to continuous effort. However, the resulting benefits to the environment, your wellness, and your finances make it an endeavor worth pursuing. Remember, every step taken towards a more sustainable kitchen is a crucial contribution towards a healthier planet.

Organizing Sustainable Storage

Transforming a traditional kitchen to a zero-waste kitchen requires meticulous planning, rearrangement, and the use of sustainable practices. This transition occurs through gradual, calculated steps rather than a quick, complete overhaul. Embracing the concept requires a mindset shift: we must become comfortable with rejecting our predisposition towards convenient, but wasteful, methods of food preparation and storage.

To commence the zero-waste journey, planning is paramount. Start by assessing your present kitchen situation. Forget about the daunting image of a perfect, waste-free kitchen for a moment, and concentrate instead on the harm that current practices may be causing to the environment. Identify kitchen activities that generate considerable waste, such as using packaged produce, disposable utensils, and plastic containers.

Next, prioritize kitchen activities that need zero-waste changes. Introduce changes gradually to enable easy adaptation and prevent the initiative from becoming overwhelming. Keep track of successful transitions to evaluate progress, reconsider actions that may not have worked well, and plan adjustments accordingly.

One key step on the journey to a zero-waste kitchen is rethinking your grocery shopping habits. Choose local farmers' markets, which often use less packaging and offer the most organic produce. One should also take along reusable shopping and produce bags to eliminate the need for plastic or paper ones.

The kitchen pantry is another area that necessitates a revamp. Gradually replace pre-packaged goods with bulk items purchased using your own containers. Switch to using sustainable storage solutions such as glass or stainless-steel containers instead of plastic ones. This transformation need not be overnight – slowly deplete your current stock, then replace it with package-free or sustainably packaged alternatives.

In this process, consider organizing your kitchen space strategically. An organized kitchen aids in minimizing food waste as you have a clear view of what is available and what needs to be consumed. Use transparent containers for easy identification of food. Regularly organizing the kitchen ensures that it stays clutter-free, reducing the chance of buying unnecessary items.

Adapting to sustainable storage is pivotal. Refrain from using plastic wrap and aluminum foil. Opt for beeswax wraps, silicone lids, or cloth covers that are reusable and eco-friendly. For refrigeration, use glass or stainless-steel containers that are not only durable and sustainable but also safe for food storage, eliminating the risk of chemical leaching associated with plastic containers.

This transition journey requires diligence, patience, and perseverance. However, the results of adopting a zero-waste kitchen – reduced waste, healthier eating habits, significant cost savings, and a minimal environmental footprint – make the effort worthwhile. As you embark on this exciting endeavor, the road may appear challenging, but remember it's about progressing, not about achieving perfection overnight. Consistent small changes eventually culminate in a significant transformation towards a sustainable and eco-friendly kitchen.

Implementing Waste Minimizing Strategies

Transitioning into a zero-waste kitchen may seem like a daunting task, but with some careful planning, organization, and the implementation of waste-minimizing strategies, you can transform your cooking space into an eco-friendly haven.

The first step is to conduct a comprehensive assessment of your current situation. This involves analyzing the amount and type of waste produced in your kitchen. By doing so, you can identify the main sources of waste and develop targeted strategies to address these issues. This audit can be as simple as keeping a diary of the waste produced over a week or as detailed as weighing and categorizing each type of trash.

Once you've assessed your situation, you'll need to start planning. This involves setting realistic goals and timelines. You cannot expect to transform into a zero-waste kitchen overnight. Break down the change into smaller, manageable steps that can be implemented over time. For example, you can start by reducing the use of single-use plastic items in the kitchen, then proceed to phase out disposable paper products, and so on.

Organizing your kitchen is another key factor in becoming waste-free. Create specific areas in your kitchen for recycling, composting, and reusing. Clear labeling and simple systems can make it easy for everyone in the household to know where to dispose of different kinds of waste. You may also want to reorganize your kitchen to make the most of storage space, resulting in less food waste due to spoilage.

Implementing waste-minimizing strategies is an integral part of becoming a zero-waste kitchen. One of the most effective ways of achieving this is by embracing the concept of mindful consumption. This involves only buying what you need, opting for products with less packaging, choosing reusable alternatives, and learning to love leftovers. Make use of modern technologies such as apps that can help residents identify compostable or recyclable materials, locate recycling centers, or plan meals.

Another strategy is to embrace home cooking and self-sufficiency. By making meals from scratch, you can avoid a lot of the packaged foods that both contribute to your waste and harm your health. Grow your herbs, or even vegetables if you have space, to reduce packaging waste and boost your diet with fresh, pesticide-free produce.

Composting is another fundamental element of a zero-waste kitchen. Collect your food scraps and turn them into nutrient-rich compost to support your garden or indoor plants. Even if gardening isn't your thing, there's likely a community compost scheme you can contribute to.

Engaging the whole household in this transformation process is crucial. Communicate your goals and plans to all household members and solicit their input and assistance. Make the zero-waste journey a collective effort that everyone can take pride in.

Remember, the goal of a zero-waste kitchen is to reduce waste, not necessarily eliminate it entirely. Don't stress if you can't achieve absolute zero-waste. Instead, make incremental changes that improve your sustainability practices over time. Be patient with yourself and others, and celebrate each step made towards becoming an eco-friendly haven.

Commitment and Mental Preparedness

Understanding the zero-waste concept

Modern living, escalated consumerism, and a lack of awareness have led us down a path of wasteful habits, having a significant impact on our environment and our health. The kitchen, being the heart of our homes, becomes a focal point where we can initiate change. The transition into a Zero-waste Kitchen is not just about replacing plastic containers with glass jars or biodegradable bags. It is a fundamental shift in our approach towards cooking, shopping, eating, and eliminating waste.

The first and crucial step towards a zero-waste kitchen involves commitment and mental preparedness. It calls for a paradigm shift from convenience to consciousness. Much like any significant lifestyle change, the transition to a zero-waste kitchen requires dedication, patience, and a steadfast resolve. A zero-waste mindset implies that you prioritize the planet over personal ease, a step that might present challenges initially. However, you should realize that it is the little everyday decisions that collectively lead to substantial environmental impact.

Understanding the zero-waste concept is the steppingstone to reimagining your cooking space into an eco-friendly haven. To effectively implement zero-waste principles, we need to learn what 'zero-waste' truly means. It's not merely about recycling or cutting down on trash; in its essence, zero-waste implies that we adopt a circular lifecycle for resources—where everything that's consumed or used can be repurposed, reused, or composted, leaving nothing to waste.

Adopting a zero-waste lifestyle means we scrutinize every aspect of our kitchen operations: from food procurement and storage to preparation and disposal. We question - How is our food packaged? How are we storing leftovers? Can the food scrap be utilized or composted? How are we disposing of the waste? By questioning every action we take, we make mindful decisions, bringing us one step closer to a zero-waste kitchen.

Engraving the principles of zero-waste into our everyday life is not an overnight process. It is a journey, often challenging, but extremely gratifying when we learn that our responsibility and actions can directly influence our environment. Every small effort counts when it comes to conserving and nurturing our planet. Through this book, we embark on a journey to equip ourselves with knowledge, strategies, and practical steps to transform our kitchen, and ultimately, our lifestyle, into one that is balanced and in harmony with the environment.

Importance of sustainable living

Embracing a zero-waste kitchen doesn't happen overnight. Making such a transition calls for thoughtful planning, strategy, dedication and most importantly, a commitment to set aside personal convenience for the greater environmental cause. This might seem like an overwhelming task, but it all begins with one step — transforming our mindset.

Mental preparedness is crucial to successfully implementing and maintaining a sustainable, zero-waste kitchen. Because let's face it, we live in a culture of disposability and convenience. Our routines, habits, and even supermarkets, are designed to supply an endless stream of disposable items without addressing the repercussions of such a lifestyle. It's ingrained in our identity, and it takes a deliberate mental shift to navigate away from this norm.

We need to start perceiving our kitchens not just as a space for cooking meals, but also as an area where we can implement conscious choices to minimize waste and promote sustainability. A zero-waste kitchen comes with a learning curve that demands continuous adaptation and resilience. It means adopting practices that at first might feel inconvenient but over time, turn into habits that are rewarding both personally and environmentally.

Emerging from this mental shift, we must emphasize the importance of sustainable living. Hinged on the principles of reducing, reusing, and recycling, it requires sourcing our foodstuffs responsibly, being cautious of our energy consumption, and avoiding as much waste production as we possibly can.

Sustainable living in the kitchen is more than just a trendy topic, it is an urgent and all-consuming approach that our planet requests of us. It urges us to integrate our waste reducing efforts seamlessly into our cooking and eating routines, taking mindful decisions that over time, become an integral part of our identity.

Indeed, every choice we make in our kitchen carries significant environmental implications. Sustainable living asks of us to be accountable for our choices, and motivates us to opt for methods and solutions that conserve the planet rather than wear it down.

In conclusion, transitioning to a zero-waste kitchen begins with a resolute mindset, persistence and an unrelenting commitment to sustainability. Remember, adopting a zero-waste lifestyle is a marathon, not a sprint. You are sure to face hurdles, setbacks and periods of self-doubt on your journey. However, every effort, no matter how small it may seem, contributes to a healthier, sustainable planet. As you start adopting these practices, you'll discover a sense of fulfillment that only comes from knowing you're making a difference in the world, one meal at a time.

Develop commitment towards eco-friendly practices

Embarking on a journey towards a zero-waste kitchen involves more than just purchasing eco-friendly products or containers. It is fundamentally a holistic approach that requires commitment and profound mental preparedness.

One must acknowledge that the transition into a zero-waste kitchen will not happen immediately, and it's perfectly fine. The goal is to gradually reduce waste production until it reaches a minimal or almost inconsiderable degree. This process demands an alteration in both perspectives and habits. Hence, the crucial and initial step in creating a sustainable kitchen is developing a commitment towards eco-friendly practices.

Commitment serves as the foundation for any long-term change. Without it, it would be challenging to break away from habitual waste production and consumption. Remember that this passage towards a zero-waste kitchen is not exclusively beneficial to our planet but is significantly advantageous to personal health and finances. When you understand and appreciate these benefits, commitment naturally sets in.

In our hectic lives, we often fall into the commonplace practices of single-use plastics, heavily packaged goods, and food waste simply due to convenience. The first hurdle we often face in transitioning to a zero-waste kitchen is breaking free from these routines, and this is where mental preparedness comes into play.

Mental preparedness is integral to this lifestyle change. It's about strengthening your mindset to accept deviations from the norm. Furthermore, it involves educating oneself about sustainable alternatives. It's essential for you to understand the impact of waste on our planet and how each person's effort can make a significant difference.

Another aspect of mental readiness is the ability to resist the allure of marketing gimmicks that push 'green products,' which might be unnecessarily costly or sometimes not as eco-friendly as they appear. Instead, you are encouraged to make conscious choices informed by research and a proper understanding of the sustainability of a product.

Remember, the journey towards a zero-waste kitchen is multifaceted and involves a gamut of emotions ranging from discomfort to elation. There might be a sense of overwhelm at first; however, with knowledge and adaptability, it becomes an incredibly rewarding and transformative journey.

In conclusion, the commitment towards an eco-friendly lifestyle and mental preparedness are key drivers in creating a zero-waste kitchen. These elements should interweave with all decisions; from restructuring shopping habits, modifying how we prepare our meals, rethinking food storage, to changing our disposal practices. Each step taken is a stride towards a sustainable world.

With willingness, understanding, and patience, the concept of a zero-waste kitchen can become a practical and achievable reality. Start today, and remember, every small change matters.

Mental readiness for lifestyle change

Transitioning into a zero-waste kitchen requires a significant shift in lifestyle; hence, it necessitates commitment and mental preparedness. The aim is to reduce the waste originating from our kitchens to zero or near zero. From changing the way we shop, cook, and tidy up, to reconsidering our need for certain kitchenware, this is a comprehensive transformation that demands mental readiness and a genuine sense of environmental responsibility.

Understanding the essence of a zero-waste lifestyle and the path to achieving one is crucial before committing to such a transformation. Zero-waste is essentially a sustainable way of living that focuses on reducing, reusing, and recycling to minimize waste production. Its success relies on anticipation and preparedness as much as it does on execution.

Before embarking on this eco-friendly journey, one must first align one's mindset with the principles of a zero-waste lifestyle. Shifting your perspective from a consumer-based mindset to a sustainability-focused one is central to this process. A zero-waste kitchen starts with you and your willingness to accept change.

Mental readiness for lifestyle change doesn't just happen overnight, it is a process. It requires getting educated about the environmental impacts of our everyday choices, becoming aware of what we consume, how we consume it and where it ends up after use. It necessitates being informed about alternatives, willing to experiment, and embracing the likelihood of trial and error.

Next is commitment. It's not enough to be informed and prepared, one needs to be committed to the cause. This involves making a resolution to persist even when it seems difficult or when the initial excitement wanes. The journey to a zero-waste kitchen is not always easy but it is always rewarding. It tests your commitment to the environment, to sustainability and to future generations.

The key is to approach this transition at your own pace. Set achievable goals, be patient with yourself, and remember that every little step counts. It's an ongoing journey of learning, adapting, and developing environmentally conscious habits.

Throughout this process, it's important to forgive yourself for mistakes or unplanned deviations. Every new habit takes time to form, and occasional slip-ups do not erase the progress you've already made. Understand that the concept of "zero" waste is a goal, and it's okay to strive for less waste instead of no waste. The true goal is to make conscious and sustainable choices to the best of your ability, guided by the overarching mission to preserve our planet.

Successfully transitioning into a zero-waste kitchen is not merely about eliminating waste; it is about nurturing an ecosystem that works for the environment, not against it. The foundation of this change lies within us, our commitment and our readiness to embrace this lifestyle transformation. It is about understanding the problem and becoming part of the solution within our own living spaces. Remember, the journey to zero-waste is not a sprint, but a marathon, where every step however small leads to a bigger impact.

Perseverance amidst early stumbles

Transitioning into a zero-waste kitchen is a journey that begins with a deep-seated commitment to sustainable living and a mental readiness to embrace fresh, eco-friendly habits. It is a definitive path towards minimizing waste generation, curbing carbon footprints, and creating an environment that nurtures one's health and wellness.

The first step to creating a zero-waste kitchen starts with changing your mindset. It is neither an instant change nor a short-term project, but a quest for gradual transformation. The ultimate goal is to shift graduate from mindless consumption towards conscious consumer behavior, which necessitate an active effort to reduce, reuse, and recycle waste.

Mental preparedness is key. It includes understanding that this process might be a bit unfamiliar and possibly daunting in the beginning. It involves learning new ways of managing your kitchen space and shopping habits, battling with the tempters of convenience, and generally adopting a lifestyle that is, many times, contrary to the one predominant in today's consumerist society.

By acknowledging these challenges, you familiarize yourself with them, which consequently helps in eliminating the element of surprise that usually accompanies trials. Knowing these, you are better equipped to handle hurdles with grace, determination, and perspective.

Perseverance plays a pivotal role in this transition. Inevitable early stumbles, such as dealing with the inconvenience of using reusable containers when shopping or forgetting to compost kitchen scraps, are common. An essential part of this journey is your ability to bounce back from such missteps, learn from them, and move forward. Think of these challenges as steppingstones that will lead you to a more sustainable way of life rather than roadblocks that deter your progress.

Remember that it's perfectly acceptable to start small. When introducing any new changes, they should be reasonable, achievable, and manageable, so as not to overwhelm you and deter you from further progress. Consider starting with one area of your kitchen, perhaps your pantry or refrigerator, and gradually expand your practices to other areas.

Lastly, be patient. Real change takes time, and every small step you take towards transitioning into a zero-waste kitchen is a significant win for the environment. Your concerted efforts towards fostering sustainability within your personal sphere of influence is a powerful act of environmental stewardship - one that behooves an intimate connection with the Earth, a profound understanding of your role within the larger ecological system, and a deep-seated respect for the planet we call home.

Execution

Start composting kitchen scraps

Transitioning into a zero-waste kitchen is not necessarily an overnight process, neither is it a change that can be brought about in haste. It requires meticulous planning, execution, and modifications to your current lifestyle. One of the critical aspects of this transition is composting kitchen scraps which can minimize waste considerably. In this guide, we delve into the steps you can undertake to incorporate composting into your daily routine seamlessly.

First, discern what can be composted. Generally speaking, any organic matter can go into the compost pile. The usual suspects include fruit and vegetable peels, coffee grounds, eggshells, tea bags, and even yard waste like grass clippings and leaves. On the contrary, avoid composting meat, dairy, and diseased plants, which can attract pests, emit unpleasant odors, and possibly spread diseases among plants.

Next, let's tackle the how of composting. Begin with selecting an appropriate compost bin that fits your kitchen space. A variety of options are available on the market, from sleek countertop models to larger outdoor versions. However, if you're handy, there are numerous DIY solutions as well that incorporate repurposed items.

Having decided on the bin, next comes layering. Start with a layer of brown material like leaves, sticks, or paper at the bottom to facilitate air flow. This is followed by a layer of green material including your kitchen scraps. Continue layering until the bin is full, always capping with a layer of brown material. Remember to occasionally turn the compost pile to aid in the decomposition process.

Bear in mind that composting doesn't translate into

immediate results. Depending on various factors like material size, compost bin design, and external temperature, it may take anywhere from two months to a year for your compost to fully breakdown. However, once it does, the reward is a fertile, nutrient-rich soil that can give life to your indoor plants or garden.

Ultimately, composting is a significant step in your journey towards a zero-waste kitchen. It is an eco-friendly practice that not only minimizes kitchen waste but also gives back to the environment in the form of nourishing soil. Committing to composting may take some effort, but the benefits, both at a micro-level in your kitchen and the macro-level on our planet, are undeniable. Remember to be patient and persistent in this journey, the end result will be worth the effort.

Swap to reusable storage

The journey to the perfect zero-waste kitchen is a gradual and rewarding process that requires intentional practice and commitment. It entails the assertion of a few adjustments not only in your lifestyle but also in your kitchen. This section aims to discuss the steps that will assist you in transitioning into a zero-waste kitchen, focusing specifically on the execution and your swap to reusable storage.

Firstly, you need to ascertain your current waste status. This involves closely examining your kitchen and its processes. This activity will give you a clear perspective of your kitchen waste contributors, thereby enabling you to develop a practical plan for reducing waste.

Once the analysis phase is over and you have identified areas that need improvement, the next step is to execute the changes. Begin by gradually reducing your dependency on disposable items such as single-use plastics, aluminum foils, cling films, and paper towels. Replace these with more eco-friendly and reusable options.

The focal point of our discussion here is the transition to reusable storage. Shifting to a zero-waste kitchen will demand changes not only in your cooking habits but also in your food storage methods. For starters, replace plastic Tupperware with glass or stainless steel containers. Glass jars of various shapes and sizes can be excellent for storing dried goods. Moreover, they can easily be reused or recycled once they have outlived their purpose.

Utilize beeswax wraps and cloth bags for your daily storage and shopping needs, respectively. Beeswax wraps serve as a sustainable alternative to plastic wraps while cloth bags can be washed and reused multiple times, negating the need for plastic shopping bags.

Besides improving waste management, a crucial aspect of a zero-waste kitchen is efficient food storage because proper storage can greatly diminish food waste. For instance, refrigeration can prolong the lifespan of different food products such as vegetables, fruits and leftovers.

Similarly, freezing particular food items is another strategy to extend their shelf lives. Nonetheless, not all food items are suited for the same storage methods. Educate yourself about these different methods to avoid incorrect food storage, which can lead to spoilage and, subsequently, increased waste.

Remember, the zero-waste kitchen evolution is a journey; it doesn't happen overnight. Start slow, allow yourself to adjust, learn from your mistakes, and celebrate your little victories along the way because every step taken towards an eco-friendly kitchen is a leap towards a sustainable lifestyle and ultimately, a healthier planet.

Choose bulk over packaging

Transitioning into a zero-waste kitchen is a journey that encapsulates various elements, key amongst which is the decision to choose bulk over packaged goods. This step signifies a shift in purchasing habits, which plays a crucial role in the overall strategy of reducing waste.

The environmental impact of packaging is a globally recognized issue. Our surfeit of packaging waste, especially plastic, has turned into a crisis. By opting for bulk purchases, we contribute to the reduction of this waste, as bulk goods usually come with less packaging, or sometimes, none at all.

Choosing to purchase in bulk is a decision that goes beyond saving the environment. The bulk buying lifestyle can benefit your pocket as well. When you buy in bulk, you can save money because the cost per unit is typically lower. It also helps reduce frequent shopping trips and thus, saves time and transportation fuels.

To successfully transition into buying in bulk, planning becomes vital. Start by identifying commodities you consume in large quantities, and you're confident won't go to waste. This could include dry goods such as grains, legumes, pasta, nuts, and spices.

Next, invest in good quality, reusable, and durable containers. These can store your bulk purchases and keep them fresh. Also, they will not add to landfill waste after one-time use, unlike non-durable containers or disposable plastic bags.

A key point to remember while transitioning is to gradually phase out buying packaged goods. You can start with a few items, then eventually add more to your bulk-buying list as you progress in your zero-waste journey. This approach makes the shift more manageable and less overwhelming.

When shopping, remember to be mindful. Zero-waste is not about buying items in bulk, only for them to go to waste. It's about careful planning and thoughtful consumption. Consider your storage capabilities and make sure you will be able to use all of the purchased items before they spoil.

Starting a zero-waste kitchen needs adopting a new mindset, with choosing bulk over packaging being a significant aspect. When we succeed in altering our shopping and consumption habits, we take a crucial step forward in reducing our environmental footprint, and journey further into becoming more conscientious, responsible global citizens.

Utilize every food part

The ethos of a Zero-waste Kitchen significantly relies upon the principle of complete usage, where every part of your food plays a crucial role. With proper execution, not only can you vastly reduce your kitchen's waste output, but also discover newfound respect and understanding for the food you consume. By ensuring you make the absolute most of what you purchase, you can gradually transform your kitchen into a sincere, eco-friendly haven.

First and foremost, one needs to become aware of what's truly edible. The contemporary kitchen has grown so accustomed to discarding certain food parts, it's often forgotten that these parts are not only edible but also tasty and nutritious. For instance, broccoli stems, commonly thrown away, can be delectably steamed, roasted or stir-fried. Bone and vegetable scraps can be simmered into rich, homemade stocks. Even seemingly inedible items such as citrus peels and apple cores can be used to make vinegar or natural cleaning solutions.

Further, minimize waste by shopping with intention. Have a solid plan before you make a trip to the grocery store. Buy only what you need and will utilize – remember, the ultimate goal is to not dispose of anything. It may initially seem challenging, but it will significantly check impulse shopping and wasteful purchases as you practice.

Maximize shelf-life by storing your food correctly. Each food item has a specific storage need that, when catered to, drastically improves its longevity. Proper food storage is a practical and fundamental aspect of reducing waste.

Enlist the help of modern technology to achieve your zero-waste goals. Many apps now exist to remind you about consumption and expiration dates, as well as give creative recipe suggestions for utilizing leftovers or Food-parts that are commonly wasted.

Finally, educate and encourage yourself as well as others. Being conscious of the environmental impact of food waste can be a huge motivator. Share your commitments with friends and family and invite them on the journey. Embody the principle of embracing a zero-waste lifestyle and become a living testament to the possibility of a sustainable living in a world driven by excess.

Achieving zero-waste in your kitchen is indeed a process, but every small step you undertake towards this ambitious goal contributes to a monumental change. With mindful execution and a steadfast resolve, your kitchen can become a symbol of sustainable culinary practices and an eco-friendly refuge in an otherwise wasteful world.

Promote home cooking

Transitioning into a zero-waste kitchen involves significant strategy and execution. The process can be divided into actionable steps that will not only foster waste reduction, but also elevate a sustainable lifestyle in terms of health, environmental impact and financial savings. A pivotal part of this process lies in promoting home cooking, which will be discussed extensively in this section.

Step 1: Assess Your Current Situation

Before diving headfirst into the zero-waste lifestyle, assess your current kitchen situation. Take note of your consumption habits, the amount of trash produced, foods that are often wasted, and appliances that may consume too much energy. Understanding your current state will provide a clear benchmark for your progress as you transition.

Step 2: Plan and Organize

Create an action plan, outlining realistic timeframes within which to achieve each stage of your zero-waste goal. This could include menu planning and shopping lists, which will prevent over-purchasing and, consequently, food wastage.

Step 3: Implement Eco-friendly Kitchen Practices

Phase out single-use items such as plastic containers, cutlery, and paper towels and replace them with reusable alternatives. Gradually transition to energy-efficient appliances and consider composting organic waste. Where possible, maintain and repair items instead of replacing.

Step 4: Inspire Home Cooking

Industrial food production contributes significantly to global waste; hence, adapting the culture of home cooking is essential in a zero-waste kitchen. Home cooking gives you full control over your ingredients, strategies for leftovers, and the opportunity to manage portion sizes to prevent waste. It also instills an understanding of the food cycle and fosters conscious eating habits.

Step 5: Committed Zero-waste Shopping

Adopt conscious shopping habits by buying only what you need. Opt for unpackaged, organically grown, locally sourced foods. Carry your own shopping bags and containers for takeaway or bulk items. This perpetuates a closed-loop system that feeds back into your zero-waste kitchen by avoiding excessive packaging.

Achieving a zero-waste kitchen is a gradual and fulfilling process. It implies a lifestyle change rather than a swift switch. With patience, commitment, and consistent effort, we can transform our kitchen into an eco-friendly haven, actively reducing our footprint on the earth while fostering our and the planet's well-being.

ESSENTIAL TOOLS FOR A ZERO-WASTE KITCHEN

Environmentally Friendly Kitchen Technology

Energy efficient cooking appliances

In creating an eco-conscious kitchen environment, one must prioritize the procurement and proper application of essential zero-waste tools alongside environmentally friendly kitchen technology.

Having a zero-waste kitchen is more than a trend or a lifestyle. It's a carefully curated journey enabled by a set of tools dedicated to achieving sustainability. A few examples to consider include silicone stretch lids that replace disposable wraps due to their durability, flexibility, and reusability. Opting for cloth napkins, instead of their disposable counterparts, reduces the waste you generate substantially. Look for utensils made of bamboo, stainless steel or any other robust, recyclable materials to further support your venture. Similarly, composting pails designed to be compact and odor-free serve as a major step towards waste reduction, while glass storage containers are an excellent alternative to non-biodegradable plastic versions due to their prolonged lifespan.

In addition to these tools, embarking on your zero-wash journey requires an exploration into environmentally friendly kitchen technology. Modern developments in technology have made it easier than ever to meld our desired convenience with eco-sustainability.

Energy-efficient cooking appliances are vital additions to your green kitchen, with designs that focus on reducing energy consumption while maximizing output. From smart fridges that can help monitor and adapt usage based on your habits, convection ovens that cook food faster and reduce energy use, to induction stove-tops that heat only the pot or pan to avoid energy wastage - every appliance matters in the journey to sustainable living.

When it comes to dishwashers, models with energy star ratings are recommended, known for using less energy and water, thus minimizing environmental impact. For small electrical appliances, consider those with automatic shutoffs, designed to save energy when not in use.

Remember, making your kitchen a citadel of sustainability is not an overnight task. It is a step-by-step process that demands patience and dedication towards the cause. We, through our conscious efforts, play a vital role in contributing to this global movement. Understanding these aforementioned essential tools and environmentally friendly kitchen technologies helps paint a broader perspective of what it takes to cultivate an eco-friendly haven right in your cooking space.

Sustainable food storage solutions

Our kitchens are the heart of our homes, places where we not only cook but socialize, create, and enjoy. As a result, they are often the places where a large part of our household waste is generated. Transitioning towards a zero-waste kitchen is not merely about reducing and eliminating waste, but also about establishing a more efficient and sustainable system that will benefit both your lifestyle and the environment.

An essential step towards this transformation involves reconsidering our tools and equipment. Let's explore the environmentally friendly kitchen technology and sustainable food storage solutions that are foundational for setting up a zero-waste kitchen.

Environment-friendly kitchen technologies are not just trendy; they are tools that can drastically minimize waste at source and are integral to your zero-waste aspirations. From energy-efficient appliances to automatic composters, technology plays a vital role in our journey towards a zero-waste kitchen. Items such as refrigerators, dishwashers, and ovens with high energy star ratings not only save on electricity but also reduce greenhouse gas emissions.

Smart kitchen gadgets like automatic composters can turn food waste into fertilizer within hours, reinforcing a kitchen ecosystem where waste is seen not as disposal material but integral to the creation of new resources. Tools like a water purifier can reduce the need for single-use water bottles, contributing to reduced plastic waste generation.

Sustainable food storage is another aspect that can make a significant impact on our waste levels. Plastics are notorious for their long degradation period and their damaging effect on the environment. Transiting to sustainable food storage involves using materials like glass, stainless steel, and silicone which are not only environmentally friendly but also healthier for us.

Glass jars are an excellent option for storing bulk items like grains and legumes, while beeswax wraps and silicon bags are ideal for storing fruits, vegetables, and leftovers. Stainless steel containers are a durable and eco-friendly alternative to plastic lunch boxes.

Our kitchen habits definitely play a significant role in our overall environmental footprint. Investing in environment-friendly technologies, appliances, and sustainable storage solutions is a step towards designing a zero-waste kitchen and creating a healthier environment for ourselves and the future generations.

Remember, the transition doesn't have to be drastic. Start small, take incremental steps, and steadily build up your eco-friendly haven. Make a commitment today to tread lightly on this planet and make your kitchen a zero-waste space. Everyone can do their part, and your kitchen is a great place to start.

Water conserving fixture options

In the quest to transform our culinary environments into sustainable, zero-waste sanctuaries, an immediate point of focus should be the tools and technology used on a frequent basis in the kitchen. Equipping your kitchen with the right tools plays a significant role in minimizing waste and creating an eco-friendly space.

The first item we will explore are those tools which form the backbone of any green kitchen - products oriented towards reducing waste. These include items such as a compost bin, reusable shopping bags, dish towels and rags to replace paper towels, glass storage containers to eliminate the need for disposable plastic, and beeswax wrap to substitute commonly used, non-degradable saran wrap.

Now, let us delve into a particular product that is rapidly gaining popularity in the eco-conscious household - the compost bin. A compost bin, whether stored indoors or outdoors, gives organic waste a new purpose. Instead of simply discarding peels, coffee grounds, and vegetable scraps - these elements can work in a compost bin and create nutrient-rich soil. Composting is a fantastic and natural way to recycle kitchen waste.

The meticulously woven threads of dish towels and rags spell out versatility. These items can dry dishes, clean up spills, and wipe down surfaces eliminating the need for the constant purchase and consumption of paper towels.

Let's take a closer look at glass storage containers. Unlike plastic, glass does not retain odor, discolor or deteriorate. This makes it an ideal choice for storing leftovers, dry food, and even liquids.

Beeswax wrap is a reusable, washable, and sustainable alternative for plastic wrap. It's perfect for packing sandwiches, fruits, and wrapping around leftovers.

Moving on to environmentally friendly kitchen technology - there is a diverse array of options available. Modern advances in technology have made energy and water efficient appliances widely accessible.

Dishwater is a prime example. Modern dishwashers are increasingly becoming more efficient, using less water and energy than traditional types. When used to full capacity, they can significantly reduce water usage compared to washing dishes by hand.

Faucet aerators can be easily attached to the kitchen sink, ensuring that less water is used by introducing air into the water stream. Additionally, it maintains the sensation of high-water pressure.

A dual flush toilet can also be incorporated into the kitchen for water conservation. The user can have the choice of two flush settings: one for liquid waste, another for solid.

Invoking these changes can undoubtedly reduce your kitchen's footprint. The revenue saved on household utilities will be a pleasant bonus to the overall feeling of satisfaction that comes with maintaining a sustainable, eco-friendly kitchen. It's not only about the transformation of physical space, but also about evolving habits and practices, leading to a lifestyle that embodies and promotes sustainability.

Recycling and composting systems

In recent years, the concept of a zero-waste kitchen, which used to be the domain of fringe environmentalists, has gained broad mainstream adoption. By transforming our cooking spaces into eco-friendly havens, we not only substantially reduce our carbon footprint, but we also can save a considerable amount of money.

The transformation begins with integrating essential tools that facilitate sustainable practices. For instance, replace single-use items with reusable alternatives. Instead of paper towels, opt for reusable cloth ones. Instead of disposable plastic bags, go for reusable glass containers or beeswax wraps. Even something as simple as using wooden spoons instead of plastic can have a long-term benefit on our environment, as they are recyclable and don't leak harmful chemicals.

Kitchen technology has also evolved to promote environmental sustainability. Modern appliances such as energy-efficient refrigerators, dishwashers, and cookers significantly curb energy consumption. Additionally, you might want to consider incorporating a food steamer into your kitchen setup. Not only do they offer a healthy cooking method, but they also consume less energy compared to other conventional methods.

Further, composter and recycling bins are also essential in a zero-waste kitchen. Start by designating separate bins for organic and inorganic waste. Organic waste like vegetable scraps and coffee grounds can be composted and returned to the earth. There are also attractive compost bins available with inbuilt carbon filters to prevent any unpleasant smells from escaping. Additionally, familiarize yourself with what you can and cannot recycle to make the most out of your recycling system.

Remember, waste isn't just about the tangible things we throw away, but also the invisible waste from energy and water. Implement touch-sensitive faucets to curtail unnecessary water flow. Not only do they save water, but they are also convenient and hygienic. LED lighting can also contribute to eco-friendly practices by consuming up to 75% less energy than conventional incandescent lighting, while lasting 25 times as long.

Assuring the journey towards a zero-waste kitchen, it's crucial to assess and invest in your individual needs and eco-goals into account. There is no 'one-size-fits-all', but every small step you take brings us closer to a sustainable planet. Ultimately, a zero-waste kitchen is not just about being kinder to the planet, it's about creating a space that reflects our values and benefits our well-being.

Biodegradable cleaning products usage

A modern kitchen involves the use of numerous tools and appliances, not all of which align with the intention of creating a zero-waste and eco-friendly space. However, if you are a responsible custodian of the earth, you can streamline your kitchen with the right sustainable tools, thus enhancing your convenience and reducing your carbon footprint.

One of the very first steps to creating a zero-waste kitchen involves selecting environmentally friendly kitchen technology. Today's market is teeming with appliances that are designed for ecological efficiency, saving both energy and resources without sacrificing functionality and performance. From energy-efficient refrigerators that keep your food fresh while minimizing power consumption, to water-saving dishwashers that clean your utensils without wasting gallons of water, there are innumerable options available. Further, induction stoves, low-flow faucet aerators and even composters are important tools for transforming your cooking space into a sustainable haven.

Equally as important as eco-friendly appliances are the tools used for cleaning up. Conventional cleaning products often contain harsh chemical ingredients that can harm the environment and pose health risks to you and your family. In order to adopt zero-waste practices in your kitchen, the switch to biodegradable cleaning products is crucial.

Biodegradable cleaning products are formulated with natural ingredients that are gentle on the environment, and yet effective enough to clean and disinfect your kitchen area. These products do not contain harmful toxins, are safe for septic systems, and they do not contribute to water and air pollution. Moreover, they often come in recyclable packaging, further reducing your waste footprint.

Moreover, you can choose to make your own cleaning products using simple and common ingredients like lemon, vinegar and baking soda. Not only does this reduce waste from packaging, but it also ensures that your kitchen remains chemical-free.

In essence, a truly eco-friendly kitchen is a result of well-thought-out choices and deliberate utilization of resources. Even seemingly small changes, such as choosing energy-efficient appliances or using biodegradable cleaning products, can significantly contribute towards creating a sustainable, zero-waste kitchen. It is important to remember that our daily choices shape our environment, and it is within our power to make decisions that protect and preserve it. Let your kitchen be the starting point of a more sustainable lifestyle.

Reusable Cooking Utensils

Choosing sustainable utensil materials

A Zero-waste Kitchen goes beyond just reducing waste, it begins with a careful reassessment of your relationship with all the products you use, from purchasing, using, to disposal. Foundational to achieving this is stocking your kitchen with items that share the same sustainable credo as your kitchen. Thus, your assortment of cooking utensils plays a big part in this transformation.

Perhaps you are questioning the need to reinvest in new kitchenware while your current ones still function adequately. This is indeed an apparent paradox: buying new in the pursuit of reducing waste. However, consider how frequently disposable products would need replacement over your lifetime compared to investing one time in sustainable alternatives. In the long run, this will save not only waste but also money.

The ideal Zero-waste Kitchen utensils share two primary characteristics: first, they are reusable, and second, they are made of sustainable materials. The durability of reusable products contributes significantly to waste reduction. It mitigates the need for constant purchasing of single-use items and the subsequent trash that follows.

However, being reusable isn't enough. The said product should also be made from sustainable materials. Plastics are ruled out in this scenario due to their environmental implications and the toxic chemicals they release, posing potential health risks. The most preferred materials include wood, stainless steel, silicone, and even bamboo.

Choosing wooden utensils, for instance, is a great sustainable choice. They are naturally non-stick and won't scratch your cookware. Wood doesn't conduct heat, so you can leave them in your pot during cooking without the handles heating up. Best of all, when they're too worn out to use, they decompose, returning to the ecosystem from where they originated.

Stainless steel is another highly durable material. It is resistant to rust, chipping, or staining, and it can withstand the test of time. It's recyclable too, meaning you can conscientiously dispose of it when it can no longer serve its purpose.

Silicon, although a synthetic material, is also a good option. It can withstand high temperatures and it's non-toxic. It's also highly versatile, meaning it can adapt to many cooking needs. Plus, it's non-abrasive, so it won't scratch cooking surfaces.

Lastly, another sustainable material is bamboo. Light, durable, and mostly organic, it's a great Eco-friendly option for various kitchen utensils.

Remember that transitioning into an eco-friendly kitchen is not instant; it is a progressive course. The goal is not to discard all your existing utensils immediately but to transition gradually, replacing items with eco-friendly alternatives as your current utensils wear out. This process requires patience, but each small step will see your kitchen metamorphose into a vibrant haven that does its part for our planet.

Durability of reusable utensils

Every gastronomic journey begins simplistically: with just a few essential tools. To transition into a zero-waste kitchen, identifying and utilizing the right set of durable, reusable cooking utensils is of prime essence.

To facilitate the process of cooking, we often tend to accumulate a plethora of kitchen gadgets and utensils over time. Unfortunately, many of these tools rarely see the light of day and contribute extensively to the waste in our kitchens. Additionally, a significant number of these tools are made from cheap plastic and other non-biodegradable materials that are harmful not just to our health but to the environment as well.

Switching to durable, reusable cooking utensils made from sustainable materials can drastically reduce environmental impact. It's important to remember that the essence of a zero-waste kitchen lies not in the absence of waste, but in the effort to limit it significantly.

Let's begin with the basics. Essential kitchen tools like a chef's knife or a cutting board need not be made from plastic. Opt for knives with stainless steel blades and wooden or bamboo handles, which lend durability and longevity. A cutting board made of bamboo or wood is a sustainable choice and often lasts longer than plastic versions, if properly maintained.

A cast iron skillet, along with a stainless steel pot and pan, should fulfill most of your cooking needs. These tools are highly durable and can last for generations if properly cared for. Replace plastic spatulas and spoons with those made of wood or bamboo. These alternatives are not only biodegradable but also resist heating better, reducing the risk of chemicals leaching into your food.

Mason jars serve as excellent storage containers, being

both reusable and recyclable. They can be used for storing everything from grains and spices to leftover food. For straining or draining, reusable muslin or cheesecloth bags can replace disposable plastic options.

Don't forget kitchen tools like a manual can opener, vegetable peeler, and grater made from stainless steel. Also consider investing in reusable, foldable shopping bags for your grocery runs instead of depending on single-use plastic bags.

Durability goes hand in hand with the choice of material and quality of craftsmanship. Opt for brands that emphasize quality, and don't hesitate to invest a bit more in kitchen tools that will stand the test of time. Most importantly, proper care and maintenance of these tools can enhance their lifespan significantly, making them truly zero-waste.

In conclusion, curating your kitchen with durable and reusable cooking utensils made from eco-friendly materials is a significant step towards realizing the vision of your zero-waste kitchen. The initial investment may seem daunting, but the long-term expenses and environmental burden is greatly reduced – a small price for a brighter future.

Maintaining reusable cooking tools

The journey towards a Zero-waste Kitchen begins with equipping oneself with the right tools and utensils that are designed to last while reducing the environmental impact. Having these essential tools in your kitchen not only allows you to cook more efficiently, but they also play a significant role in minimizing waste produced in your cooking space.

Let's begin with the Triple R - reduce, reuse, and recycle - of kitchen utensils. Instead of disposable plastics, opt for long-lasting materials such as stainless steel, glass, and wood. These materials are not just sturdy and durable, but also lend an appealing aesthetic to any kitchen space.

Invest in a good set of stainless steel pots and pans. Stainless steel is not only durable, but it also does not leach harmful chemicals into your food, making it a healthier choice as well. Cast iron skillets are another excellent investment that can last for generations if properly cared for.

A good set of knives is indispensable in all kitchens. Opt for high-quality knives that can be sharpened and maintained for years, rather than disposable ones. Look for knives with handles made of durable materials like wood or metal.

Replace your plastic bowls and containers with glass or metal variants. Not only are they safer to use, but they are also easier to clean and can withstand heat, cold, and pressure without releasing hazardous substances.

Let's not overlook the importance of reusable cooking implements, notably, spatulas, spoons, and tongs made of wood or metal. Unlike their plastic counterparts, they do not melt or deform and are safe to use with all sorts of cooking vessels.

Lastly, consider using reusable baking mats and silicone

covers, which replace the need for wasteful foils and plastic wraps.

Maintenance of these reusable cooking tools is just as crucial as their selection. Regular and thorough cleaning ensures they stay in a good state, increasing their utility and lifespan. For wooden and metal utensils, avoid soaking them in water for prolonged periods, and always dry them properly to prevent rust and decay.

Stainless steel items can be cleaned and polished with natural ingredients like vinegar and baking soda, avoiding the need for chemical-laden cleaning agents. Similarly, cast iron cookware should be seasoned regularly to maintain its non-stick properties and prevent rusting.

In conclusion, the transition to a zero-waste kitchen is not a complex process. The first step involves replacing disposable, plastic tools with reusable, long-lasting ones, and caring for them properly. By doing so, we can significantly reduce both our ecological footprint and our individual exposure to harmful toxins. Remember, each little step towards sustainability counts. Your zero-waste kitchen journey can start today.

Cost-effectiveness of reusable utensils

In our journey towards sustainable living, the kitchen is an essential place to begin. Equipping it with the right tools can help to conserve resources, save money, and bring us closer to the ideal of a zero-waste home. Translated into kitchen terms, the zero-waste concept encourages us to shift our mindset from a purely economic perspective to one that balances financial needs with ecological considerations.

When it comes to cooking tools, this often means opting for reusable over disposable options. While disposable items may seem convenient, they contribute to increasing amounts of waste and often end up accumulating in our rivers, oceans, and landfill sites. In contrast, reusable cooking utensils, though demanding an initial investment, can save money in the long run while significantly reducing waste output.

Investing in sturdy, long-lasting tools is the cornerstone of an eco-friendly kitchen. A good set of stainless steel pots and pans, wooden spoons, silicone spatulas, and a high-quality chef's knife could last decades if cared for properly. Ceramic or glass baking dishes, stainless steel strainers, and reusable baking mats can replace their disposable counterparts, further reducing waste.

Similarly, common kitchen consumables can be replaced with reusable alternatives. For example, instead of relying on disposable paper towels, consider buying a collection of washable dishcloths. Say goodbye to plastic wrap and welcome beeswax wrap into your repertoire of kitchen tools. Instead of plastic sandwich bags, opt for reusable silicone bags.

Yet another consideration is how to handle waste when it does occur. Composting is a fantastic way to manage organic waste like fruit peels, vegetable cuttings, and used coffee grounds. By composting, we actively contribute to the circle of life, turning food scraps into a nutrient-rich supplement for plants and gardens. Pair composting with a robust recycling system, and we can notably decrease what we send to landfills.

While it's evident that reusable kitchen tools have a higher upfront cost than their disposable counterparts, the long-term cost-effectiveness is clear. The average household spends a significant amount annually on disposable goods that can easily be replaced with reusable alternatives. Though making the switch requires an initial investment, the cost-savings over time, along with the positive environmental impact, make this a worthwhile consideration.

Transitioning to a zero-waste kitchen isn't about perfection. It's about making as many small changes as you can to reduce the waste you produce. Sustainable living is all about creating a healthy balance between economic and ecological considerations. By implementing reusable utensils and tools in our kitchen, we're taking a significant step in the right direction. The journey is ongoing, but every step counts.

Ethical buying and manufacturing

In pursuit of a zero-waste vision for your kitchen, it's not only the food that matters but also the tools you use for preparing and serving it. The utensils, appliances, and dishes that we employ in our cooking endeavors all contribute to the environmental footprint generated from our kitchens. To have an eco-friendly kitchen, it's important to arm yourself with reusable tools that are ethically sourced and manufactured.

Seeking sustainability from the get-go requires making thoughtful choices on the tools we bring into our kitchens. It's essential to prioritize quality over quantity, longevity over disposability, and ethical sourcing over mindless consumption.

Reusable cooking utensils form an integral part of a zero-waste kitchen. When choosing your cooking tools, instead of grab-and-go plastic utensils that degrade over time and often can't be recycled, opt for more durable materials like stainless steel, wood, or bamboo. By choosing reusable utensils, you can effectively cut down on the number of single-use utensils that would eventually end up in the landfill.

Moreover, the consideration of how these appliances and utensils are manufactured is crucial. Nowadays, more and more manufacturers are adopting environmentally friendly practices to curtail pollution and minimize waste. Before purchasing, do your research to find brands that champion sustainable manufacturing procedures and ethical labor standards. This means looking for companies that produce minimal waste during production, utilize renewable resources, refrain from using harmful chemicals, and ensure fair and safe working conditions for their employees.

When it comes to dishware, for example, locally made ceramic plates and bowls may be a preferable choice to mass-produced plastic ones. Similarly, glass or stainless-steel storage containers are ideal replacements for single-use plastic bags and boxes.

Lastly, craft a habit of maintaining your cooking utensils properly. Reusing is just half of the equation; making sure that reusable items last as long as possible is the other half. Caring for your tools effectively prolongs their lifespan, helping you save money and reduce waste in the long run.

By consciously choosing reusable and ethically produced cooking utensils, you're driving the demand down for single-use kitchenware and reducing your own carbon footprint. Remember, transformations don't occur overnight, the shift to a zero-waste kitchen starts with one small step in the right direction. Being aware of what we buy, where it comes from, and how it was made equips us with the power to effect change.

Containers and Storages

Reusable glass containers importance

In the pursuit of a zero-waste kitchen, having the right set of tools is indispensable. Among these essentials, the importance of containers and storage cannot be overlooked. They are the backbone of an eco-friendly kitchen making it possible to store, transport, and utilize food efficiently without contributing to landfill waste.

Among the varying container options, reusable glass containers stand out for their versatility, longevity, and health advantages. They are of cardinal importance in our quest for a zero-waste cooking and eating space.

For starters, glass containers are easily reusable and remarkably durable. Once bought, they can serve their purpose for many years, unlike their plastic counterparts which often need frequent replacing. This not only lessens the need for future purchases, therefore reducing waste, but also presents economic advantages.

Additionally, the environmental implications of glass surpass just the reduction of waste. Glass containers are fully recyclable, meaning at the end of their lifespan - which can be quite extensive - they can be transformed into new products without losing purity or quality. This process can play out infinitely, leading to substantial reductions in raw material usage and emission of CO_2.

Apart from environmental benefits, reusable glass containers present significant health advantages. Unlike certain plastics, which can leach harmful chemicals into your food, glass is chemically inert. This means it does not react with the food or drinks stored in it and ensures that your meals are contaminant-free. This is especially important when storing acidic or hot foods which increase the risk of chemical leaching in plastic containers.

Furthermore, from a practical perspective, glass containers are arguably more comfortable to use. Their transparency allows you to see what's inside them without the need to open and check, saving time, and ensuring better organization of your kitchen space.

It is true that the initial investment in glass containers may be higher than that of acquiring plastic ones. However, the long-term benefits certainly outweigh this initial cost. Investing in a set of these essential tools is undoubtedly a worthwhile step towards transforming your kitchen into an eco-friendly haven.

To conclude, focusing on the tools at our disposal, with an emphasis on containers and storage, is an integral part of the journey to a zero-waste kitchen. Prioritizing reusable, recyclable, and health-friendly materials such as glass containers is an environmentally responsible and economically savvy way to jumpstart this transformative journey. With these minor adjustments, our kitchens can become the forefront of a sustainable lifestyle revolution.

Stainless steel storage solutions

Successful transformation of your kitchen into a zero-waste haven requires thoughtful re-evaluation of the tools and products you currently utilize. The journey to sustainability does not necessitate elimination but strategic replacements and adaptations with an ultimate goal: no waste. In this context, the value of containers and storage solutions, particularly those made from stainless steel, cannot be overstated.

Stainless steel is a non-toxic and non-leaching material that reliably resists rust and damage over time. It's entirely safe for food storage – an essential characteristic for kitchenware – and offers the durability missing in plastic variants. The longevity of stainless steel containers ensures they're not swiftly delegated to the landfill. Not to mention, it's corrosion-resistant properties keep them in impeccable condition even after extended periods, making them an excellent long-term investment.

An illustrative feature of stainless steel kitchenware is its versatility. From storing your bulk-bought grains and legumes to preserving your left-over dinner, a stainless steel container has diverse applications. They hold a particular charm for maintaining food's temperature, making them equally useful for keeping your soup warm or your ice cream cool.

Another notable advantage of stainless steel is its ability to withstand high and low temperatures. You can use these containers in refrigerators, ovens, or even on stovetops without risking damage to the vessel or the contents inside. Unlike their plastic counterparts, they don't release harmful chemicals when exposed to heat, preserving your food's genuine flavors and maintaining the kitchen's overall safety profile.

Stainless steel containers are easy to clean, ensuring no residual or lingering smells. Moreover, they don't stain or absorb food colors, making them ideal for storing different types of food items.

Stainless Steel storage solutions impeccably merge an environmentally friendly approach with aesthetics. The sleek, modern, and minimalistic designs of these containers harmoniously blend with the contemporary kitchen decor while fulfilling a core sustainability goal.

From an eco-conscious perspective, stainless steel also promotes reducing, reusing, and recycling. Once you've comfortably utilized your stainless steel containers for years and they've reached their end of life, they can be completely recycled. This repurposing aspect makes stainless steel a truly zero-waste material.

In conclusion, stainless steel storage solutions embrace practicality, aesthetics, convenience, and most crucially, sustainability. As the chase for zero-waste lifestyle gains momentum, the steel container rises as a hero; it's high time to acknowledge their compelling prospects and consider them as an integral part of an eco-friendly kitchen.

Recycled plastic containers usage

In the journey to manifest a zero-waste kitchen, tools play a quintessential role. Among these, the most fundamental are containers and storage solutions. These items, when chosen wisely, can contribute significantly to reducing waste, ensuring practical functionality, and enhancing the aesthetic charm of your cooking space. Let's delve deeper into how we can optimize the use of containers and storages in the context of a zero-waste paradigm, with special emphasis on the usage of recycled plastic containers.

Containers and storage units in a kitchen, whether big or small, are the nexus of organization. They house everything from our dry goods and leftovers to utensils, allowing us to systematize our kitchen for efficiency. When moving towards a zero-waste kitchen, it becomes especially pivotal to choose containers that are durable, reusable, and above all, made of sustainable materials. Glass containers are a popular choice, given their durability and lack of harmful chemicals. However, recycled plastic containers should not be overlooked.

The feasibility of recycled plastic containers resides in their ability to give a second life to what would otherwise be waste, thereby reducing our carbon footprint. These containers, made from post-consumer plastic, can be employed similarly to their conventional plastic or glass counterparts. They are versatile, lightweight, and often come in an array of sizes to accommodate different storage needs. Their usage can effectively help mitigate plastic pollution by encouraging recycling and plastic reusability. Hence, such an eco-friendly option must be valorized.

However, a mindful approach needs to be adopted when integrating recycled plastic containers into your zero-waste kitchen. Not all recycled plastic is safe for food storage. It is prudent to look for containers made from type 2 (HDPE) or type 5 (PP) recycled plastic. These types of plastic are generally considered the safest for contact with food. In addition, ensure that they are free from Bisphenol A (BPA), a chemical often used to harden plastic that can seep into food and cause numerous potential health effects.

Moreover, recycled plastic containers should be manipulated carefully to prolong their life and reduce the need for replacement. Avoid exposing them to extremely high temperatures as this can lead to warping or releasing of plastic residues. For cleaning, use mild soaps as abrasive detergents can scratch the surface, making it more likely to retain bacteria.

In conclusion, with careful selection and thoughtful handling, using recycled plastic containers can become a cornerstone in the transformation of your kitchen into an eco-friendly haven. They help reduce our collective reliance on virgin, single-use plastics while simultaneously promoting a circular economy. Indeed, your zero-waste kitchen would stand incomplete without these eco-conservative receptacles.

Bamboo lids and cases

The heart of a zero-waste kitchen lies in the diligent selection and utilization of sustainable tools that promote waste reduction, and prime among these are eco-friendly containers and storage items. Whether it's eliminating single-use plastics or favoring materials that are easily recyclable and sustainably produced, the transition to a zero-waste lifestyle starts with reconsidering the receptacles we use to hold and store our foods. With this in mind, let's explore the role of containers, storage items, bamboo lids and cases in shaping a zero-waste kitchen.

Containers form the front line of the waste-reducing movement in any kitchen. They act as alternatives to plastic wrap and disposable bags, providing the perfect solution for storing leftovers, packing lunches, and even grocery shopping. The push towards using containers starts at the supermarket, where you can bring your reusable containers to purchase items from the bulk foods section. This not only decreases packaging waste but can also save you money as bulk items are often cheaper than their packaged counterparts.

Storage items in a zero-waste kitchen aren't exclusively limited to containers; they also comprise of canisters, jars, and bags made from sustainable materials like stainless steel and glass. These items ensure the longevity of food items and help reduce food waste—a significant contributor to greenhouse gases. For instance, produce bags made from eco-friendly materials like organic cotton are perfect for storing fresh vegetables in the fridge while glass jars work excellently for dry goods such as cereal, grains, and pasta.

On a similar note, bamboo lids have emerged as an excellent eco-friendly alternative to plastic counterparts. Naturally antimicrobial, lightweight, and biodegradable, these lids often complement glass or stainless-steel containers, enhancing their longevity and functionality. They are an excellent solution for reducing both the use and disposal of plastic lids that often end up in landfills, thereby lowering your environmental footprint.

Lastly, bamboo cases serve as sustainable replacements for plastic utensil holders or cutlery trays. Aesthetically pleasing and exceptionally durable, bamboo cases offer the perfect blend of elegance and sustainability to a zero-waste kitchen. They are an eco-friendly answer to storing and organizing kitchen utensils, making your kitchen space clean and orderly while keeping it green.

In the grand scheme of things, the journey to a zero-waste kitchen isn't solely about swapping plastic for sustainable alternatives. It's an ongoing process that involves understanding why we produce waste and conscientiously practicing habits that reduce and ultimately aim to eliminate it.

In conclusion, to establish a green, eco-friendly haven takes more than just recycling—it requires us to be deliberate in our selection, be it containers, storages, bamboo lids, and cases. Each element we choose brings us a step closer to achieving a zero-waste kitchen that respects and aligns with Mother Nature's equilibrium. These seemingly simple changes can play a significant role in lowering our carbon footprint, thus paving the way for a more sustainable future.

Wax wraps for leftovers

Finding innovative solutions to reduce waste in the kitchen is the first step towards truly embracing the principles of a zero-waste lifestyle. Transforming your cooking space into a haven of eco-friendly practices begins with investing in the right tools, containers, and storage methods that promote sustainability.

Every kitchen has its unique set of tools and materials that aid cooking and storage processes. However, the key to establishing a zero-waste kitchen lies in selectively choosing items that are not only long-lasting and reusable but also contribute to minimizing environmental damage.

One of the major wastes produced in the kitchen is from packaging. Using durable, reusable containers can effectively curb this issue. Consider investing in glass containers or stainless steel ones, which are not only more durable and long-lasting than their plastic counterparts, but also safer for storing food. These materials do not leach harmful chemicals into your food and can be cleaned easily. They also come in various sizes, catering to your diverse storage needs, be it freezing, refrigerating, or storing dry goods.

Another innovative tool that has emerged in the zero-waste kitchen space is the wax wrap. These reusable, washable, and compostable wraps are designed to protect and preserve food, replacing the conventional single-use plastic wraps. Wax wraps are made from cotton fabric coated in a thin layer of beeswax, tree resin, and often a few drops of jojoba oil.

This unique composition gives them a similar flexibility and adhesive quality as plastic wrap, making them perfect for covering leftover food items and storing them safely without the risk of air exposure. Not only does this maintain the freshness of the food for longer, but it also helps to avoid food wastage. Moreover, these wraps can be washed and reused multiple times, contributing significantly to a reduction in kitchen waste.

While the wide world of zero-waste tools and storage options might seem overwhelming at first, starting small, say with reusable containers and wax wraps, can make a significant difference. Remember, the objective is to slowly transform your kitchen into a more mindful space that respects and prioritizes sustainability – a goal that, with mindful efforts and small, consistent steps, is more achievable than you might think.

FOOD SHOPPING FOR A ZERO-WASTE KITCHEN

Buying in Bulk and Unpackaged Foods

Advantages of bulk buying

Investing time and thought into the process of shopping for your kitchen can drastically reduce the production of waste, while simultaneously promoting an eco-friendlier lifestyle. Crucial to the Zero-waste Kitchen paradigm is a shift in purchasing habits—specifically directing attention towards buying in bulk and opting for unpackaged foods.

Buying in bulk is not a foreign concept; it has been around for centuries. However, its value in the fight against waste is not as widely recognized as it should be. Opting for bulk purchases enables consumers to buy the exact quantities they require, thereby significantly reducing waste at the source. This method of shopping also cuts down on the use of unnecessary packaging that often accompanies smaller-portioned goods.

In order to shop in bulk, arm yourself with reusable containers such as glass jars, Tupperware, or cloth bags. These can be used to stow goods such as grains, pasta, cereals, dried fruits, and nuts directly from bulk bins. Not only can this drastically decrease the amount of plastic and paper waste generated in the kitchen, but it also lends itself to a more organized cooking space.

Concurrent to bulk buying is the preference for unpackaged foods. This primarily applies to fruits, vegetables, and other fresh produce. Instead of selecting pre-packaged options enclosed in plastic wrap or containers, choose loose, fresh produce. Besides creating a reduced waste footprint, this also provides an opportunity to select the best quality products —each tomato can be studied for ripeness, each apple for firmness, enhancing the quality of meals prepared.

Bulk buying and choosing unpackaged foods come with notable cost advantages too. Often, unit prices for bulk purchases are lower than those for smaller-portioned options. This implies extensive savings in the long run. Furthermore, buying unpackaged vegetables and fruits exempts us from paying a premium for the packaging convenience.

In conclusion, shifting to bulk-buying and selecting unpackaged foods, at the very least for a majority of shopping needs, can result in significant waste reduction. Additionally, it can lead to healthier meals, a cleaner kitchen, and considerable cost savings. It is these small changes that pave the path towards a Zero-waste Kitchen. One needs only to embrace these practices with an open mind and a firm resolve to transform their cooking space into an eco-friendly haven. Remember, every great journey starts with that first tiny step. Here, it begins with a smart, eco-friendly shopping habit.

Locating local bulk stores

In today's rapidly industrializing world, adopting sustainable practices is no longer a novel idea; it's a pressing requirement. Harmonizing the melting pot of diverse cuisines that our kitchens often turn into, with the concept of zero-waste, may seem like a daunting task. Yet, with small but sure steps, we can pave the way to a greener future in the very heart of our homes - our kitchens.

One such sustainability stride starts with an often-overlooked domain – food shopping. Contrary to popular belief, eco-friendly shopping doesn't indulge in compromises, but instead indulges in a more responsible form of consumption that is both efficient and beneficial for our wallet.

Buying in bulk is a convenient and cost-effective way to begin. Not only does this approach reduce waste generation through lesser packaging, but it also empowers us to buy exactly what we need, no more, no less. Buying in bulk also reduces the cost per unit of the items we purchase, making it a financially rewarding practice as well. However, while opting for larger quantities, pay special attention to ensure the food items won't spoil before they can be fully utilized.

Bulk buyers can make significant strides toward reducing waste by bringing their own reusable containers or bags to transport and store their food. Some food stores will also permit shoppers to use their own containers, further reducing reliance on single-use plastic and paper bags.

Choosing unpackaged foods is another essential wrinkle of zero-waste shopping. While this may sound limiting initially, do bear in mind that a substantial portion of everyday groceries, including fruits, vegetables, meats, and dairy are traditionally sold unpackaged. If that isn't a feasible option, seek out food items that come in recyclable packaging.

Speaking of recycling, one more way to transform your kitchen into a zero-waste haven is by sourcing your groceries from local bulk stores. Local bulk stores provide opportunities to buy everything from grains to spices in as much quantity as required, reducing both waste and unused food. Moreover, buying local goods means less carbon footprint since the goods haven't traveled long distances, thereby generating fewer greenhouse gases.

Taken together, these steps towards zero-waste food shopping can have a profound impact on individual efforts to lessen landfill loads, reduce their carbon footprints, and cultivate a more sustainable lifestyle. While the journey to a zero-waste kitchen may sound challenging, it is a rewarding endeavor that has the potential to transform our cooking spaces into an eco-friendly haven, and above all, pave the way for a brighter, greener future. Remember, change always begins at home.

Storage solutions for bulk foods

The concept of a Zero-waste Kitchen begins at the very heart of our food ecosystem - shopping. In contrast to traditional grocery shopping methods that often result in vast amounts of waste from packaging, proponents of a zero-waste lifestyle advocate for two primary shopping practices: buying in bulk and choosing unpackaged foods.

Buying in bulk eliminates the superfluous packaging involved in individually wrapped items while often saving money. Think of necessities such as rice, beans, pasta, and spices. Even certain vegetables and fruits, like potatoes and apples, can be bought in bulk. These easily stored staples are perfect zero-waste choices, providing both financial savings and environmental impact reduction.

Choosing unpackaged foods goes hand-in-hand with buying in bulk but also extends to everyday grocery shopping. Think of the unnecessary plastic wrapping around cucumbers or the excessive Styrofoam and plastic coverings for meats. Instead, consider selecting fresh, loose produce and using reusable mesh bags. The butcher counter can easily place your chosen cuts directly into your own containers, eliminating the need for disposables.

Although these shopping practices dramatically reduce waste, they also create a new challenge: storage. Our modern kitchen storage solutions are all too often geared towards packaged goods. But with a few simple adjustments, we can easily adapt to store our bulk and unpackaged foods.

For dry goods, consider using glass jars or containers. Not only do they provide an airtight seal to keep foods fresh, but they also allow easy visibility of their contents, making meal planning and inventory checks a breeze. Perishable items, such as produce and meats, can be stored in reusable silicone bags, beeswax wraps, or glass containers in the fridge. As for bulk items, cloth bags and large metal tins, or even a dedicated pantry if space allows, can be the perfect, easy-to-access storage solutions.

In a Zero-waste Kitchen, every step of the process, starting from shopping to cooking to storing, is an opportunity to make mindful choices towards sustainability. Not only can these steps save you money, but they also cut down on excessive waste, effectively helping you reduce your carbon footprint while creating a healthier kitchen environment for you and your loved ones.

Reducing packaging through bulk buying

The concept of a zero-waste kitchen begins with taking the steps towards mindful purchasing, specifically when it comes to your food shopping habits. Shopping practices exert significant influence on the production and disposal of waste, which can counter the principles of a zero-waste kitchen if not managed with a meticulous plan.

The power to direct our consumption towards sustainability lies right in the hands of consumers, especially when it comes to buying in bulk. This concept is not an entirely innovative one - making it all the more easily applicable. Historically, buying in bulk has always been a proven strategy for both cost-effectiveness and sustainability. The core essence of bulk buying lies in purchasing larger quantities of products, eliminating the need for individual packaging for each item. This subsequently reduces the amount of waste material that can quickly accumulate in the average household kitchen.

However, the implementation of bulk buying requires a balance of practicality and conscious decision making. The benefits of this method manifest through minimal waste production, but it is also important to avoid overconsumption. A strategy must be developed to prevent food wastage born from spoilage, which inherently counters a zero-waste initiative. Incorporate sturdy, reusable containers in your shopping routine which can be filled directly from bulk bins. The correct way to adopt this purchasing method lies in buying an appropriate amount of food that can be consumed within its freshness period.

Buying unpackaged foods presents another triumphant strategy in creating a zero-waste kitchen. This approach promotes the use of reusable and refillable containers that you can take to local grocery stores or farmers' markets. Not only does this mean you are actively eliminating excessive packaging waste, but you are also supporting local economies and businesses that champion sustainable practices.

However, it is crucial to recognize that buying entirely unpackaged food is not always feasible. It can be challenging to find every product without packaging, from dairy products to certain types of fresh produce. It becomes vital to make the best choices possible given one's circumstances, like choosing products in glass or paper packaging which are recyclable and less harmful to the environment than plastic.

The efforts to decrease packaging through bulk buying and purchasing unpackaged foods is a journey of remodeling habits and embracing a mindful shopping routine. The transformation into a zero-waste kitchen should be gradual and thoughtful, taking into account the delicate balance of minimizing waste and maintaining a nutritious and diverse food diet. Remember, the goal is not perfection but progressive, consistent strides towards waste reduction. Your kitchen is a powerful starting point to reshape waste management in your household, nurturing a better environment for the future generations.

Sustainable shopping habits

The transformation from an ordinary kitchen to a zero-waste haven begins in the most unexpected place - the grocery store. The process of selecting and purchasing our food significantly impacts the level of waste output in our kitchens. Therefore, it's crucial that we paint a clear picture of what sustainable grocery shopping looks like.

The path to zero-waste shopping entails a shift in our shopping habits to more conscious and eco-friendly options, with a focus on two primary strategies - buying in bulk and choosing unpackaged foods.

Bulk buying does not necessarily mean purchasing large quantities of food. When we speak of bulk buying in the context of zero-waste, we refer to the practice of buying food without any packaging. Many grocery stores have sections dedicated to bulk goods such as grains, legumes, nuts, seeds, spices, or even some forms of produce. By using reusable containers or cloth bags, you can access these resources without contributing to unnecessary waste. This practice not only minimizes the excessive packaging of individual products but also allows you to gain monetary savings in the long run.

Meanwhile, opting for unpackaged foods further reduces the production of plastic waste associated with single-use packaging. Plastic packaging often ends up in landfills or, even worse, in our oceans, corroding aquatic life. In selecting unpackaged fruits and vegetables, not only are you minimizing your contribution to the waste pandemic, but you are also making healthier eating choices.

However, this shift towards sustainable shopping habits doesn't merely focus on how we shop but also where. Prioritize local farmers' markets and stores that encourage bulk buying. Not only do these establishments support zero-waste initiatives, but shopping locally also curbs carbon footprint due to reduced transport emissions.

The zero-waste kitchen philosophy extends far beyond our cooking space. It challenges us to rethink our shopping practices and make conscious choices that encourage sustainability. Remember, every sustainable decision, no matter how small, supports the wider initiative of transforming your cooking space into a zero-waste haven.

Choosing Local and Organic

Embrace local farmers' markets

The concept of creating a zero-waste kitchen begins long before entering your kitchen and standing in front of your stove. It starts when you step out for food shopping. The choices you make here significantly influence the amount of waste you produce and the overall environmental footprint of your kitchen.

When embarking on the journey towards a zero-waste kitchen, one must reevaluate their purchasing habits and consciously choose local and organic. Choosing locally grown food helps reduce your carbon footprint, as it involves shorter transportation chains and less packaging while also supporting local farmers and the local economy. Furthermore, locally grown food typically tastes better because it is fresher and grown in its natural season.

Organic farming is both eco-friendly and sustainable. Aside from contributing to the health of our planet by maintaining soil fertility, reducing pollution, and conserving biodiversity, choosing organic encourages a reduction in the use of hazardous chemicals. Organic farming safeguards groundwater quality and ensures safer, purer produce in our kitchens.

Embracing local farmers' markets is an effective way to implement both local and organic purchasing habits. These markets provide fresh, organic produce straight from the farm. Shopping at local farmers' markets not only enables you to reduce plastic packaging waste but also allows you to interact directly with growers. By conversing with our farmers, we can gain a deeper understanding of where our food comes from, how it was grown and what practices were used—information typically absent in the fluorescent-lit aisles of grocery stores.

Choosing local and organic does not mean limiting your food choices. Instead, it encourages you to eat a more seasonal diet, which allows you to diversify your plate and nutrition. Concurrently, you are reducing waste, global warming potential, and plastic pollution, making a big stride towards your zero-waste kitchen.

In conclusion, conscientious food shopping is the cornerstone of a zero-waste kitchen. Rethinking your food shopping habits and choosing local and organic are transformative steps towards an eco-friendly haven.

Not only does this choice promote a sustainable and healthy lifestyle, but it also paves the way for a safer and more secure food future.

Purchase seasonally available food

Employing a zero-waste strategy in our kitchens requires making significant changes to our everyday shopping habits. A successful transition entails shifting our focus from the dominant supermarket culture towards more enlightened forms of acquiring our food. This includes an emphasis on local, seasonal, and organic food purchases.

Shopping locally plays a critical role in the journey towards a zero-waste kitchen. When we purchase local food, we promote the reduction of waste originating from packaging and transportation. It's important to remember that every mile our food has to travel increases its environmental footprint, in consequence of the energy consumed and the emissions produced during its transportation process. By prioritizing local produce, we decrease our food's carbon footprint, support our local economy, and also enjoy the benefit of fresher, nutrient-rich food.

Incorporating organic food into our meals signifies another important change we must make. Organic farming practices are kinder to the environment, as they don't introduce toxic pesticides and synthetic fertilizers into the soil and water systems, thereby promoting a healthier ecosystem. Furthermore, they're free from genetically modified organisms (GMOs) and are high in antioxidants and other beneficial nutrients. Though organic food might sometimes be more costly, it's worth noting that the health and the environmental benefits outweigh the extra dollars spent.

However, to truly achieve a zero-waste kitchen, we also need to pay heed to seasonality when making our food purchases. To understand why, we need to grasp that out-of-season ingredients often travel great distances, meaning their carbon footprint is high. In sharp contrast, seasonal food reduces the energy needed for growing, harvesting, storing, and transporting. Besides, seasonally available food is more likely to come from local sources, consequently reducing waste further. Seasonal food also offers the added advantage of being fresher, hence tastier and more nutritious.

In conclusion, the path towards a zero-waste kitchen incorporates three pivotal shopping habits—prioritizing local food, opting for organic, and purchasing food according to the natural cycles of the seasons. This not only aids in the reduction of waste in our kitchen but also contributes to promoting a healthier overall environment while supporting local economies and boosting the nutritional value of our meals.

Consider organic food options

In your pursuit of a zero-waste kitchen, the first, and perhaps the most crucial step, starts not within the kitchen itself, but rather from where you source your ingredients - the supermarket, local stores, or farmers market.

Today's food supply chains, unfortunately, contribute significantly to waste generation, often due to over-packaging, transportation, and the discard of imperfect produce. Therefore, conscious, mindful shopping plays a crucial part in your zero-waste journey.

Choosing local and organic produce allows us to counter these wastage patterns. Locally sourced fruits, vegetables, and other commodities reduce the need for extensive packaging and long-distant transportation, a primary contributor to pollution. By purchasing locally, we support local farms and small businesses and encourage sustainable farming practices by linking the economy directly with ecology.

Organic produce is another integral part of a sustainable shopping strategy. Organic farming practices are created with a vision to work in harmony with nature, without the use of chemical fertilizers, pesticides, or genetically modified organisms. Consequently, there's a positive impact on soil health, ecosystems, and individuals' well-being. An added advantage of organic farming is the sequestering of carbon in the soil, which helps to combat climate change.

Nevertheless, it's essential to navigate carefully the world of organic labels. Not every item marketed as organic reflects true organic farming practices. Familiarize yourself with certifying bodies and look for their logos when you shop. Furthermore, always keep an eye on the origin of your organic produce, as the closer it is to you, the more sustainable it is likely to be.

Accountability and mindfulness during food shopping are

steps towards achieving your zero-waste kitchen objectives. Choosing locally sourced, seasonal, and organically grown food provides solutions that not only impact the environment positively but also cater to healthier dietary choices. Remember, reducing waste doesn't stop at recycling or composting. It extends further to incorporate every aspect of our lives, starting from how we shop to how we eat.

Transitioning to a zero-waste lifestyle is more than merely making a change—it's about recognizing the global impact of our daily decisions and our role in the interconnected web of sustainability. It's about ensuring that our kitchen isn't just a hub of nourishment for us, but also for the planet we inhabit.

Analyze transportation footprint

Food shopping is an essential component of every kitchen's functionality and every household's sustainability agenda. By choosing local and organic, we can significantly contribute to the transformation of our kitchens into eco-friendly havens. This choice, however, extends beyond mere preference; it encompasses a holistic understanding of the environmental implications of our purchasing preferences, specifically the concept of transportation footprint.

Transportation footprint refers to the total volume of emissions—expressed in its carbon equivalent—emanating from the transportation of goods. Every product we consume has a transportation story that impacts its overall footprint. It is, therefore, crucial to buy fresher, nutrient-dense products that, hopefully, have not traveled very far. The less distance your food has to travel to reach your plate, the smaller its transportation footprint. This helps lower carbon emissions, which play a significant role in greenhouse gas expansion and global warming.

This is where local and organic foods come in. Buying locally, preferably from farmers' markets or food cooperatives, means consuming foods that have been produced within smaller radius. Besides being fresher and often organic, these goods require less transportation, reducing their environmental impact. Local farm produce also tends to be less packaged, eliminating wastage from unnecessary wrapping or plastic.

Organic farming, on the other hand, rejects the use of synthetic pesticides and fertilizers, preserving the soil's integrity and biodiversity. Unlike traditional agriculture, it does not deplete but nourishes the environment, producing foods that are healthier and more nutritious.

However, we understand that local and organic foods may not

always be accessible or affordable. This is no cause for worry or guilt. Should that be the case, it is vital to prioritize foods that are in season, minimally packaged, and produced as close as possible to your location. This way, even if your foods are not strictly 'local' or 'organic', you still maintain a sustainable, low-waste kitchen.

Finally, let's not forget reusable shopping bags, bulk buying, and thoughtful planning. These actions further reduce kitchen waste and contribute to a more sustainable and eco-friendlier environment. Together and in moderation, the sum of our combined efforts will create the change we aspire to – one zero-waste kitchen at a time.

In essence, the key to actualizing a zero-waste kitchen lies in our everyday choices. By being conscious consumers and understanding the greater symbolism embedded in our food purchasing behavior, we can transform our kitchens—and, by extension, our homes—into spaces that are in harmony with the Earth.

Support community-supported agriculture

Embarking on a journey towards a zero-waste kitchen necessitates a shift in how we approach food shopping and consumption. This doesn't just mean cutting down on packaging or recycling more efficiently; it involves a holistic rethinking of where our food originates, how it's grown, and the process it undertakes to reach our tables. A key strategy lies in choosing local and organic produce.

Food that travels across countries, or even continents, has an enormous carbon footprint attached to it. These 'food miles' consist of the greenhouse gases emitted throughout the food's transportation. Contrarily, locally sourced food not only aids in reducing these emissions but also in increasing local biodiversity and promoting healthier soils as a by-product of sustainable farming practices. Therefore, supporting local farmers and growers is essential to ensuring the food system's reduced impact on the environment.

Moreover, when choosing local, there's a higher chance you are buying fresh produce that doesn't require preservatives or excess packaging to increase its shelf life - a significant step towards a zero-waste kitchen. That being said, it falls to reason that choosing organic is an equally essential aspect of sustainable food shopping. Organic farms promote diversity and maintain ecosystems, enhancing the quality of produce and reducing the reliance on harmful chemicals and pesticides.

Organic produce is also often fresher, having faced fewer transportation strains than non-organic food sources. It's a healthier, tastier alternative that goes hand in hand with a zero-waste lifestyle. Naturally, organic and locally grown food comes with a higher price tag due to the labor-intensive nature of these practices, but every purchase serves as an investment, not only in our health but also in the health of our planet.

This brings us to the concept of community-supported agriculture. These programs are a win-win for both farmers and consumers. Consumers receive a regular supply of fresh, local, and typically organic produce, while farmers get financial support and assurance that there is a market for their output. By subscribing to such a program, not only will you ensure your financial investment supports sustainable farming, but you'll also significantly reduce the waste produced by food packaging, as many community-supported agriculture programs use reusable containers or zero packaging.

Overall, shopping for a zero-waste kitchen is an intentional act. It is deliberately choosing local, organic, and supporting community-based agricultural initiatives. This conscious choice comes with a multitude of rewards - better tasting, fresher food, supporting local economies, protecting the environment, and most importantly, reducing waste, bringing us several steps closer to our ultimate goal: The Zero-waste Kitchen.

Smart Grocery Shopping

Choosing bulk over packaging

Having a zero-waste kitchen starts long before any food preparation takes place - it begins at the grocery store. The choices you make when shopping have a significant impact on the generation of waste in your kitchen. With this in mind, approaching food shopping with a zero-waste mindset will not only transform your kitchen but also your lifestyle, as it forces us to be mindful consumers.

Smart grocery shopping is one of the most effective ways to attain a fully sustainable kitchen. Primarily, it involves making conscious decisions on what to buy, how it is packaged, and how much of it is necessary. When shopping, it is crucial to ask yourself the following questions: Is this item packaged in a way that will generate waste? Is there a more sustainable alternative? Can I buy this in bulk? Is the amount I'm purchasing more than I can consume?

Choosing items with less packaging is a simple switch with a significant impact. Often, the most challenging part of waste reduction in the kitchen is dealing with inescapable packaging. However, by opting for fresh produce over pre-packaged fruits and vegetables, you fundamentally decrease the amount of plastic that goes into your kitchen bin.

Moreover, even dry goods like pasta, rice, legumes, and spices often come in single-use plastic bags or non-recyclable cardboard boxes. Favor stores that offer loose/bulk options where you can bring your containers. If you can't find these items in bulk, look for options that use recyclable or compostable packaging.

When considering bulk buying, it's not about purchasing more than you need to reduce packet waste. Instead, it's about buying just the right amount, but with less packaging. Bulk purchasing allows you to reduce packaging waste and the frequency of shopping trips, saving you both time and money.

Shopping with a precise list helps avoid impulse buys and unnecessary food waste. Before going shopping, plan your meals ahead and list the ingredients you will need. This prevents overbuying and consequent waste.

Adopting the above practices makes a massive step towards cultivating an eco-friendly kitchen. It might feel challenging and inconvenient at first, but, like all lifestyle changes, it becomes more comfortable with practice. Remember, the goal is progress, not perfection. Spreading the process out and incorporating one change at a time can make the transition less overwhelming and more sustainable.

A zero-waste kitchen is not just about reducing, recycling, or repurposing waste. It's about fostering a sustainable mindset, thinking about our consumption patterns, and making conscious decisions that prioritize the environment. The changes you make in your kitchen will not only reduce waste, but also create a healthier, more cost-effective living environment. So, let's begin this journey - your eco-friendly haven awaits.

Utilizing reusable shopping bags

The journey towards a zero-waste kitchen goes beyond just meal preparation and plate scraping. It is inherently rooted in our shopping habits, the selections we make at the supermarket, and indeed, how we transport those selections from store to home. With this in consideration, let's dive into the concept of food shopping for a zero-waste kitchen, which encapsulates smart grocery shopping and the crucial usage of reusable shopping bags.

The cornerstone of zero-waste food shopping is predicated on smart, thoughtful grocery shopping. Planning and preparation are your most powerful tools in this regard. Before you find yourself roaming the stainless-steel valleys of your local supermarket, take a moment to accurately analyze what you truly need. Constructing a well-thought-out shopping list based on actual needs, rather than impulsive wants, significantly reduces the chances of purchasing unnecessary items which may likely end up as waste.

Furthermore, making all-encompassing shopping trips at less frequent intervals reduces the carbon footprint associated with travel. As you shop, you aim to select items with minimal to no packaging, opting for whole foods over processed variants, and procuring products housed in recyclable containers instead of disposable plastics. Bulk stores that allow you to dish out products into your own reusable containers can be quite beneficial, helping you avoid unnecessary packaging all together.

Now, having discussed smart grocery shopping, it is imperative to emphasize an often overlooked yet fundamental method of curtailing waste – using reusable shopping bags. Unfortunately, it is far too common to accumulate an unnecessary number of plastic bags during grocery shopping, most of which find their final resting places in our oceans or over-flowing landfills.

Reusable shopping bags are an eco-friendly alternative to traditional plastic and paper bags, benefiting both the environment and the consumer. By keeping and reusing them each time you shop, you curtail the demand for new bags, directly reducing waste. Not only are they sustainable, but they are also more durable and can withstand more weight than their plastic counterparts.

The move to reusable bags is not just a personal choice. It's a pivotal move towards an eco-friendly haven that prioritizes sustainable living by promoting a healthier environment. Remember, every bag counts, and every choice we make contributes directly to the future of our planet.

By adopting smart grocery shopping habits and consistently utilizing reusable shopping bags, you are not only transforming your kitchen into an eco-friendly haven, but also proactively contributing to global sustainability. A zero-waste kitchen is achievable; it begins with better choices, conscious living, and a sustained commitment to eco-friendly practices.

Supporting local farmers markets

In our quest to establish the zero-waste kitchen, understanding buying patterns is paramount. The practice of food shopping plays an essential role in this narrative. Smart grocery shopping not only minimizes food waste but also influences the production and consumption practices that have a direct impact on our environment. As such, smart grocery shopping for a zero-waste kitchen extends beyond our homes to the larger community, with a significant focus on supporting local farmers markets as an essential practice.

The premise of smart grocery shopping lies in conscious purchasing decisions -buying only what you need. By planning meals ahead, you can effectively list down the exact quantities of ingredients required, thereby avoiding any unnecessary purchases that often lead to waste. Furthermore, remember to check your fridge and pantry before visiting the store. This aims to eliminate any potential overstocking of items that may result in spoilage or excessive packaging waste. Shopping with reusable bags and containers is another fundamental strategy to radically reduce single-use plastic and afterwards any waste.

Equally important in the journey to ensure zero-waste is supporting local farmers markets. Besides being one of the key strategies of sustainable living, shopping at local farms plays a comprehensive role in the overall functionality of the zero-waste kitchen.

Firstly, fresh produce purchased directly from farmers markets often comes without excessive plastic packaging involved when shopping from regular supermarkets. This not only alleviates the stress of dealing with unnecessary waste but also ensures a healthier, package-free food intake.

Secondly, locally grown produce means reduced food miles.

By curtailing the distance that food travels from farm to our plates, we significantly lower the amount of carbon emissions associated with its transport.

Lastly, supporting local farmers markets fosters a meaningful connection between the consumer and the producer. This relationship enhances the consumer's understanding of the food source, raising awareness about the importance of sustainable agriculture and its role in environmental conservation.

In conclusion, transforming your kitchen into a zero-waste haven necessitates a rethink of our food acquisition practices. Transitioning to smart grocery shopping and supporting local farmers markets can significantly effectuate the desired reduction in waste, placing us on a rewarding path towards an eco-friendly cooking space.

Opting for seasonal produce

The journey towards an eco-friendly lifestyle begins long before any food graces your kitchen countertops. It commences at the point of purchase- during your grocery shopping. Making your kitchen zero-waste fundamentally involves re-thinking your shopping habits and the choices you make when picking out your food items.

Start with the simple yet transformative act of taking your own bags to the grocery store. By avoiding plastic bags, you immediately tie in with the principle of reducing waste. Furthermore, this practice grows into a habit with ease and time, making it a useful change that sticks and scales to other areas of your life.

Moving forward, the heart of an eco-friendly lifestyle throbbing within your kitchen's walls beats vigorously for local, seasonal produce. These food items are a beautiful means of embodying sustainability in your day-to-day living. Not only do they contribute to waste reduction by circumventing unnecessary food transportation miles and harming plastic packaging, but they also guide you towards healthier and more vibrant eating habits, thereby enhancing your personal well-being.

Seasonal produce often has a natural abundance and is typically fresher since it hasn't endured long storage periods. As a result, it is richer in flavor and nutrients in contrast to out-of-season, imported equivalents. In buying and consuming such fruits, vegetables, and other food items, you make a knowledgeable choice to support your local farm economy. This sustains smaller-scale, often organic farming methods, reducing the harmful impact of large, industrial agricultural practices on our environment.

On a more practical level, it is worth realizing that becoming acquainted with your area's local, seasonal yields can direct your meal planning and prepping efforts. You keep your menu rotating with diversity, freshness, and excitement. After all, sustainability and zero-waste living do not necessarily equate to a dull, monotonous lifestyle. Indeed, it is an opportunity to explore new ingredients, support local businesses, and enjoy the rich flavors of food as intended by nature within the appropriate season.

So, before you step foot in the grocery store, remember that you hold the power to cause positive ripples into the environment through your choices. Smart grocery shopping isn't complicated—it's about reducing waste, wisely choosing what you buy, and where you buy it from. Commence this journey, and you will transform your cooking space into an eco-friendly haven while promoting a healthier lifestyle.

Avoiding overly packaged goods

The journey towards creating a zero-waste kitchen starts outside of the home – specifically, at the grocery store. Your shopping habits significantly influence the amount of waste produced in the kitchen, making it imperative to cultivate smart, eco-friendly grocery shopping tactics.

The fundamental aim for zero-waste food shopping is to select items with minimal to no packaging and to use reusable containers or bags to carry these purchases. The modern food supply chain is notorious for unnecessary packaging - plastic-wrapped produce, canned goods, boxed meals, and non-recyclable plastic bags are a few examples of this persistent problem. However, with a bit of attention and effort, it is possible to shop in a way that minimizes and even eliminates this source of waste.

Begin your intentional food shopping journey at the produce section. Opt for loose fruits and vegetables as opposed to those pre-packaged in plastic bags or shrink-wrap. Carrying your own reusable mesh or fabric bags can serve as a handy alternative to the plastic bags commonly found in this section. Similarly, if given the choice, select the larger fruit or vegetable. Not only does this typically mean better value for money, but it also reduces the surface area exposed to potential injury, extending its useful life.

In the grains, beans and seeds aisle, try and source bulk suppliers. Stores that provide bulk goods allow you to fill your reusable containers directly, eliminating the need for packaging. If this is not an option, aim for larger packaging rather than single-serve packs to reduce the ratio of packaging to product.

Packaged goods are inevitable in some instances. For example, sauces, condiments, and specific perishable foods such as dairy products and meats. In these cases, opt for packaging that can either be reused or is more easily recyclable. Glass jars and metal cans are great options as they can often be reused or recycled more efficiently than plastic containers.

Finally, refuse the classic plastic grocery bag. Instead, bring your own reusable bags, boxes or baskets. Not only can these carry more weight, but they also significantly reduce the plastic waste that ends up in landfills or, worse, our waterways.

Transforming your kitchen into a zero-waste haven isn't a mission that can be completed in one day, rather it's a journey that involves adjustments to habits maintained over time. Smart grocery shopping is a crucial step in this journey. Undertake this endeavor one shopping trip at a time, and soon enough you'll see your kitchen waste dwindle.

FOOD PREPARATION IN A ZERO-WASTE KITCHEN

Zero-waste Cooking Techniques

Bulk shopping for ingredients

The Zero-waste Kitchen starts with adopting the right mindset towards food preparation, targeting the heart of the matter literally – cooking techniques and shopping habits. One principle of zero-waste living is the conscientiousness of our actions, being aware of our environmental footprint in all we do, including cooking. The courage to change is the first step in transforming any kitchen into a zero-waste haven.

Food preparation in a zero-waste kitchen is an art and science. It starts with meal planning, which allows you to not only decrease food waste but also save time and resources. A weekly meal plan allows you to list out the ingredients needed, eliminating the prospect of impulse buying, over-purchasing, or duplicating items already available in your kitchen. It's essential to get creative with your leftovers as well; reusing them in interesting ways can lead to delicious surprises and evoke a sense of resourceful opportune.

Next, let's delve into the techniques and practices which are unique to zero-waste cooking. From using every part of the food, including the bits often thrown away, to cooking in bulk to save on energy waste, these are the strategies that will set your kitchen apart in its eco-friendliness. For example, vegetable peels can serve as composting material or flavor stocks and broths, while overripe fruits can be transformed into smoothies or desserts. Chicken bones can be used as the base for a nutritious soup. The possibilities of a no-waste kitchen are boundless; every morsel contains potential if we adjust our lens to perceive it as such.

Moreover, the manner in which we procure our ingredients can significantly contribute to our zero-waste goals. Bulk shopping not only decreases packaging waste but also the carbon footprint associated with multiple shopping trips. When bulk shopping, remember to bring your reusable containers and bags, and only purchase the quantity needed. Shopping from local markets and farmers also supports community economies and reduces the carbon footprint linked with transportation. Remember to favor seasonal produce; it generally uses fewer resources to grow and delivers high nutritional value.

As has been made clear, each step of the way – from planning, preparation, to procuring – can be transformed to resonate with the philosophy of a zero-waste kitchen. With creative tips and tricks, the eco-friendly haven you wish to establish within your cooking space will not just be profitable to the environment, but also satisfaction to your soul and palette. This may require a deeper level of thoughtfulness and little adjustments in your day-to-day practices, yet rest assured, each small step you take towards zero-waste makes a lasting impact.

Using reusable storage containers

Understanding the nuances of sustainable cooking is an integral component of maintaining a zero-waste kitchen. The process of eliminating waste begins with the way we select and prepare our food, so as to minimize the strain we place on our environment. By adopting a zero-waste approach to cooking, we can fundamentally reevaluate and markedly improve our utilization of resources.

Central to zero-waste cooking techniques is the appreciation for all ingredients and the optimization of their use, placing importance on minimizing waste through adopting practical and efficient practices. To practice zero-waste cooking, it is essential to reduce the amount of processed food we buy and consume. Packaged and processed foods are generally characterized by their excess packaging and their environmental footprints. As a result, investing time in preparing meals from scratch can be one of the most impactful changes we can make.

Food preparation begins with mindful purchasing. Choosing loose fruits and vegetables over pre-packed ones reduces packaging waste. Buying in bulk is another effective way to reduce waste generation, as it allows the use of reusable containers, eliminating dependency on single-use plastic bags. Moreover, sticking to specified shopping lists can counteract overbuying, resulting in less food wastage.

Apart from mindful purchasing, adopting innovative cooking techniques can play an important role in waste reduction. We can repurpose parts of food typically discarded - peels, stalks, or bones, for instance, can be transformed into flavorful broths or compost for our gardens. Such creative uses not only reduce waste but also help extract the maximum value possible from the food we consume.

Moreover, the appropriate storage of food can significantly impact waste outputs. The use of reusable storage containers is invaluable in any zero-waste kitchen. They can be used to store leftovers and bulk-bought food, reducing the need for single-use packaging materials like cling film or aluminum foil. Glass jars, metal containers, and beeswax wraps are all eco-friendly alternatives that can keep your food fresh while minimizing your contribution to landfills.

The process of transitioning to a zero-waste kitchen is not an overnight conversion, but rather a journey of learning, understanding, and implementing. It requires habitual changes and conscious decisions in everyday culinary practices. With each step in the right direction, we are becoming better stewards of the planet while enhancing our culinary experiences in our very own eco-friendly haven. Remember, every bit counts, be it saving a single plastic bag or using every part of the vegetable; each action matters in the journey towards a zero-waste kitchen.

Optimizing energy-efficient appliances

In the concept of Zero-waste Kitchen, food preparation crests the vital implication of sustainability through adept utilization and minimal production of waste. A myriad of zero-waste cooking techniques have emerged as poignant strategies in transforming our kitchens into eco-friendly havens. Transitioning towards these techniques is not a daunting task; it just necessitates small tweaks in our regular cooking habits.

From purchasing to processing, every phase of food preparation can be smartly maneuvered to curtail the generation of waste. Ensuring we purchase in bulk, opting for packaging-free stores, and leveraging locally sourced produce are some fundamental strategies to begin with. When it comes to cooking, it's integral to reinvent our methods to align with the zero-waste principles.

One efficient approach is meal planning in advance. This paves the way for optimized use of ingredients, inhibits impulsive buys, and proficiently helps in mapping out portions, preventing any excess that eventually leads to waste. Further, the tactic of "root to stem" cooking is worth incorporating. Emphasizing using every part of the fruits or vegetables not only curbs waste but also introduces us to inventive recipes. Vegetable peelings, for instance, can be repurposed into nutritious broths instead of being discarded.

Another powerful resource at our disposal is our kitchen appliances. Optimizing their usage for energy efficiency is an art in itself. For most meals, oven cooking can be replaced with a slow cooker, which consumes comparatively less energy. Similarly, fully loading the dishwasher before running it saves substantial water and energy.

Furthermore, the refrigerator is the hotbed where most of our waste occurs. Incorporating an effective fridge-management system is a significant step towards a zero-waste kitchen. A simple step is to keep the items nearing their use-by-date at the front of the fridge to ensure they get used.

In essence, if we view through the lens of sustainability, waste is not waste unless we waste it. Embracing energy-efficient appliances and cooking techniques, combined with conscious efforts towards minimizing food waste, we can mold our kitchens into models of sustainability. As we tread this path, we will find that the essence of a zero-waste kitchen lies not in the pursuit of perfection, but in the pursuit of making small, intentional changes that have profound impacts. Let's redefine and revolutionize our kitchen spaces to enhance their role as harbingers of sustainable living.

Composting organic kitchen waste

The uninitiated might ask: how does one navigate the realm of gustatory creation without leaving behind the usual collateral damage? The answer to that is as delectable as it is sustainable: through a zero-waste approach.

Food preparation in a zero-waste kitchen emphasizes the principle of mindful utilization. It starts from the purchase of raw ingredients to the disposal of peelings or leftovers. The idea of minimal to zero-waste may seem lofty in a domain where everything from an onion peel to a meat bone can be considered as waste. However, adopting a strategic and educated approach can convert what one considers as 'trash' into culinary 'treasure'.

In zero-waste cooking, understanding the unique qualities and potential of each ingredient serves as a preliminary step. For instance, the stock derived from vegetable trimmings or the marrow from leftover bones can form the basis of a nutritious and flavorful soup. Similarly, overripe fruits can still find their raison d'être in baked goods or homemade preserves. The concept rejects a superficial or hasty understanding of usability as it encourages thorough use of each ingredient, extracting as much value as possible.

The art of pickling, fermenting, and drying also plays a significant role in a zero-waste kitchen. These age-old preservation practices do not only reduce food waste by elongating usability, but they also provide a plethora of health benefits and enrich the overall cooking repertoire with an array of flavors.

Composting, in essence, forms the backbone of circular economy in a zero-waste kitchen. It involves the recycling of organic kitchen waste, transforming heaps of food scraps into a rich soil supplement, also known as 'black gold'. Composting contributes to waste reduction, but it is perhaps its positive effect on soil fertility and carbon footprint reduction that makes it a major facet in the narrative of sustainable cooking.

The trajectory of sustainability in the kitchen does not only recharge the relationship we have with food but challenges our creativity as well. Competitive consumption imbibes respecting the cycle that food goes through — breaking it down makes it easier to understand the role that we play in it. Through zero-waste cooking, we are mitigating our environmental footprint, economizing our resources, and telling a story — all in the humble confines of a kitchen. Lastly, the zero-waste journey teaches us an invaluable lesson about respecting our environment: sustainability is satiating — both for us and for our planet.

Meal planning to prevent waste

The Zero-waste Kitchen is a paradigm shift in our conventional approach to cooking and food preparation. It incorporates not only the choice of eco-friendly products but also takes into account the changes we need to make to our cooking and food preparation habits. The primary goal is to create a sustainable environment that reduces waste to an absolute minimum or eliminates it entirely. Achieving zero-waste in your kitchen involves three primary areas of focus: food preparation, cooking techniques, and meal planning.

In terms of food preparation, a zero-waste kitchen requires mindful shopping. The first step is buying only what you need to reduce food waste as much as possible. This means planning your meals ahead, and doing a proper inventory of what you have and what you need. Buy in bulk whenever possible and choose to carry your own jars and containers. Opt for fruits and vegetables that are unpackaged and prefer loose options over pre-packaged ones.

When it comes to cooking techniques, introduce methods that prioritize using every part of your ingredients. This includes root-to-leaf cooking (using all parts of your vegetables and fruits) and nose-to-tail cooking (using all parts of an animal). In addition, you can save and use cooking water for soups and sauces, ferment scraps, and turn vegetable ends and peelings into broth. Embrace preservation techniques like pickling and canning which can increase the longevity of your food, thereby helping you achieve zero-waste cooking.

Meal planning is a crucial aspect of a zero-waste kitchen. It is essential to develop a weekly meal plan and stick to it. The practice can significantly reduce impulsiveness when shopping and cooking, and thus help cut down on waste. Every time you plan, take inventory of what you already have in your pantry and refrigerator and incorporate those into your meals. Plan to make dishes where you can use leftover parts or scraps from other meals. For example, a bone leftover from a roast chicken can provide the basis for a rich stock or leftover vegetables can be used in stir-fries or soups.

Nobody gets everything right from the start, but it's important to make a start, nonetheless. Even small changes like refusing disposable plastics, reducing food waste, reusing containers, and recycling, can make a big difference in bringing us closer to the goal of zero-waste. The objective of committing to a zero-waste kitchen is not just about reducing waste, but about respecting resources, respecting the environment, and putting a value on food as nourishment. Through this guide, we hope to put you on a path of less waste and more taste.

Recipes for Reducing Food Waste

Embracing Leftovers Creativity

The core objective of a zero-waste kitchen is not only to redesign the cooking space into an eco-friendly haven but also to rethink the very concept of culinary practice itself. Many of us seldom evaluate the extent of waste that stems from everyday cooking. From unconsumed portions casually tossed out to the overlooked utility of certain food parts, waste is a persistent element in our kitchens that often goes undiscussed. So, let's talk about making a switch to an environmentally friendly habit of cooking and consuming food.

To kickstart the transformation into a zero-waste kitchen, it's crucial to emphasize planning and preparing meals in ways that prevent food loss. Start by adopting simple measures such as understanding what sits in your fridge and pantry. Basing your meal plans on these existing items aims to avoid extra shopping and consequential waste. Proper storage methods also play a key role in maintaining the freshness and extending the life of your fruits, vegetables, and other perishable products.

Embracing frugality in the kitchen is a strong step towards achieving a zero-waste target. This includes creating recipes that can minimize food waste. Consider 'root-to-stem' or 'nose-to-tail' recipes that utilize every part of an ingredient – these can make your dishes more innovative and nutritionally diverse, while also reducing waste. For instance, the vegetable peels you would normally dispose of can be repurposed to make stock, and the bones from cooked meat can be boiled into a flavorful broth.

Leveraging leftovers is, indeed, an art that can be mastered with creativity and a bit of enthusiasm. Leftovers are valuable resources and give you the opportunity to be resourceful and innovative. Whether it's incorporating yesterday's salad into a refreshing smoothie, using leftover soup to cook rice or creatively using roast chicken scraps in sandwiches or salads; the possibilities are only as limited as your imagination. Expanding your cooking repertoire to include such techniques can drastically reduce food wastage and also provide your meals with a unique touch.

Food waste in the kitchen is not merely a matter of environmental concern, but a reflection of our attitudes towards the resources we so often take for granted. Implementing methods to minimize food waste, adopting resource-friendly recipes, and embracing leftovers in creative ways are fundamental parts of the zero-waste kitchen. Changing the cooking culture to be more mindful and respectful of the ingredients we use, we can make our cooking spaces eco-friendly, while also carving a path towards a more sustainable future.

Versatile Stock Soup Mastery

In the zero-waste kitchen, the value we place on ingredients parallels the respect we afford for our environment. Therefore, a crucial aspect of food preparation in such a kitchen is utilizing every fraction of the ingredients available to us. This is, without doubt, an essential strategy in combating food waste.

Contrary to what many people assume, cooking with this mindset does not limit your culinary creativity. Instead, it urges us to think beyond established norms and discover new and delicious ways of blending flavors. It equips you with the ability to transform what was once considered waste into something mouthwatering and nutritious.

Take, for instance, vegetable peels, stems, and leaves often discarded without a second thought. These 'scraps' hold immense flavor and nutritional value, only needing the right recipe to showcase their potential. The same applies to parts of meat often thrown away. The bones, skin, and fat may not seem appealing at the first glance but cooking them properly will not only help you reduce food waste but will also add an incredible depth of flavor to your dishes.

One such recipe that perfectly embodies this concept is the versatile stock soup.

Mastering the art of making stock soup allows you to turn your kitchen scraps into something delicious and wholesome. The ingredients for this are flexible, allowing you to accommodate anything from vegetable peels, mushroom stems, herb stems, onion skins, to chicken or beef bones, meat trimmings, fish heads, etc. The method couldn't be easier. All you need is a slow simmer and a little bit of patience. As the stock cooks, it extracts all the flavor it can from the ingredients, infusing the liquid with a rich, full-bodied taste. Once strained, you have a nutritious base that can be used for a multitude of dishes.

What's more, homemade stock is an economical and healthier alternative to store-bought ones, which often come loaded with sodium and preservatives.

In conclusion, food preparation in a zero-waste kitchen isn't merely about changing our cooking habits. It is about embracing resourcefulness and creativity, while also acknowledging the value of the ingredients we use and an urgent need to respect our environment to secure a sustainable future. So, as we continue this journey towards a zero-waste kitchen, let our mantra be: 'Cook wisely, waste nothing'.

Seasonal Ingredient Maximization

Having a zero-waste kitchen implies adopting a comprehensive, sustainable approach to food preparation. This involves several changes to the way we traditionally view cooking, ingredients, and waste in our homes.

Food waste is a monumental challenge. According to the United Nations, roughly one-third of all food produced globally ends up as waste. This isn't just a gross misuse of resources; it's an environmental issue, as decomposing food emits methane, a potent greenhouse gas. The zero-waste kitchen counters this problem by focusing on a root-to-stem approach to food preparation.

In root-to-stem cooking, every part of a vegetable or fruit is utilized in a way that is flavorful and nutritious. Done properly, it can be a journey of new taste sensations. Take broccoli, for instance. While the florets are the most commonly used, the stem and leaves are equally delicious and packed with nutrients. The stems can be spiralized into noodles or thinly sliced into a salad, while the leaves can be blanched or sautéed.

In the framework of reducing waste, the concept of leftovers also changes. Leftovers are not re-heated meals; they are ingredients for a new recipe. Vegetable peels can be used to make vegetable broth, while yesterday's roast chicken can be today's chicken salad sandwich or tomorrow's chicken broth.

Coming to the point of recipes, it's essential to reframe how we view them. Even the most experienced home cooks rely on recipes, but zero-waste cooking necessitates flexibility. Get comfortable with substituting one ingredient for another or even leaving out something if you don't have it. The key is to get creative with what you've got, aiming to maximize ingredients and minimize waste.

One practical way to minimize your kitchen waste is by

maximizing your use of seasonal ingredients. Seasonal fruits and vegetables are often abundantly available and tend to be fresher and less expensive. By aligning our menus with the calendar, we can make the most of each season's bounty, save money, and simultaneously slash our carbon footprint as seasonal produce requires less energy for storage or transportation.

In conclusion, a zero-waste kitchen is not achieved overnight. It's a journey that will require you to rethink your relationship with food. But the reward is not just a more sustainable planet. This approach can lead to more innovative, flavorful dishes and may even save time and money. It's an exploration worth embarking upon, transforming your cooking space into an eco-friendly haven by making calculated, conscious choices every day.

Perfection in Portioning

The kitchen is the heart of every home; a nucleus of nutrition where delicious meals are made. While the process of cooking can be a delightful venture, it becomes even more rewarding when we take conscious steps towards reducing waste. Every effort spent in reducing waste not only contributes to a healthier environment but also provides a gratifying feeling that we are doing our part to preserve the planet for future generations.

Having a zero-waste kitchen does not entail a drastic overhaul of your lifestyle, but calls for a shift in habits, particularly in three main areas: food preparation, utilizing recipes that help reduce food waste, and achieving perfection in portioning.

Food preparation largely contributes to waste in numerous ways. The routine processes of peeling, chopping, rinsing, and disposing of certain parts of ingredients often lead to unnecessary waste. One of the first steps towards a zero-waste kitchen lies in re-evaluating how we prepare our food. This includes considering whether parts of the ingredients normally discarded can be used and exploring different cooking methods. For instance, instead of disposing of vegetable peels, they can be used to make nutritious broth, while fruit scraps can serve as sweeteners for homemade jams or pies, or even ferment into vinegar.

In line with reducing waste, reimagining our recipes is instrumental. Mindful cooking involves using ingredients in their entirety or finding ways to integrate leftovers into another meal. We all have some food items that we end up never using and they eventually go bad. The key is to be creative; many ingredients can be used more extensively than we are accustomed to, and many leftover meals can become part of a completely new dish.

Lastly, the often-overlooked aspect of portioning plays a pivotal role in establishing a zero-waste kitchen. It's not uncommon to prepare too much food, resulting in leftovers that often don't get eaten. Ideally, cooking should correspond to the number of portions required. Over time, through trial and error, portioning can become an intuitive process that significantly reduces food waste. We can eliminate the problem of excess by learning to cook only what we need.

In conclusion, creating a zero-waste kitchen isn't as daunting as it sounds. By rethinking food preparation, creatively transmuting recipes, and mastering portion control, our kitchens can beautifully metamorphose into eco-friendly havens. Not only will these practices contribute to a healthier planet, but they also introduce us to a wider array of tastes while saving money by making the most of what we have. So why not start today? The journey into a zero-waste kitchen is one delicious step towards a sustainable lifestyle.

Comprehensive Composting Techniques

In today's modern age, sustainable living isn't just a trend; it's a necessary step towards protecting our planet. One of the key contributors to daily waste is often overlooked – our kitchens. Adopting a zero-waste policy within our kitchens can dramatically reduce our carbon footprint, promote a healthier lifestyle, and ultimately, save us money. This revolution begins with rethinking our attitudes towards food preparation, understanding recipes that reduce food waste, and mastering comprehensive composting techniques.

Food preparation is intimately interwoven with waste generation, cutting across the prepping, cooking, and post-meal stages. However, a shift in perspective and approach can transform this high waste generating activity into a minimal or zero-waste process. Techniques like using the whole of produce - vegetables, fruits, poultry, fish, and meats - are critical. For example, vegetable peels can be used for making stocks and broths, and chicken bones and leftovers can be turned into nourishing soups. By practicing thoughtful meal planning and portion control, we can significantly reduce food waste whilst ensuring a balanced, nutritious diet.

In line with the zero-waste philosophy, understanding and executing recipes that help to minimize wastage is equally important. Numerous delicious dishes can be created from ingredients that are often carelessly discarded, and these recipes can help instill a sense of respect for the produce we consume. Overripe fruits can be used in smoothies, jams, and baked desserts. Stale bread magically transforms into crunchy croutons or a decadent bread and butter pudding. The possibilities are endless, simple, and satisfying.

Using your kitchen scraps to create compost is another fundamental process, turning what would have been waste into a resource instead. Composting isn't necessarily a complicated process. Start by segregating your kitchen waste into two categories: the 'greens' (e.g., vegetable and fruit scraps) and the 'browns' (e.g., leaves, branches). Once segregated, layer them alternatively in a compost bin or heap, making sure to aerate the pile periodically. Introducing composting worms speeds up the process. Over time, this waste will decompose into a rich, fertile compost that can significantly improve the quality of your home garden soil.

In conclusion, integrating the zero-waste ethos in our kitchens involves conscious efforts in food preparation, adoption of waste-reducing recipes, and proper composting. These changes may seem daunting initially, but with patience and practice, they become second nature. Our kitchens can then finally stop being a part of the problem and start being an important part of the solution.

Meal Planning and Leftovers

Understanding Meal Prep Advantages

The Zero-waste Kitchen necessitates a fresh approach towards meal planning and handling leftovers, an extensive part of which is understanding the advantages of meal preparation. This concept goes beyond the simplicity of being organized, stretching into an eco-friendly lifestyle that influences both our physical well-being and the well-being of the environment around us.

One of the primary pillars of a Zero-waste Kitchen is extensive meal planning. Many tend to view this as restrictive; however, meal prep comes with flexibility and a wide array of options while fostering a waste-free environment. It is an organized system where the primary goal is to ensure maximum utilization of all purchased ingredients for the week or the month.

The benefits enveloping this minimal-waste living approach are endless, starting with the reduction of food waste. By planning your meals, shopping becomes a task that caters to your exact needs. You do away with the impulsive purchases of ingredients that might not be necessary and could potentially end up as waste.

Meal prep also saves time and reduces stress. Imagine a scenario where each mealtime does not involve the scramble of figuring out what to cook followed by the daunting task of preparing it. A well-planned weeks' worth of meals cuts down on hours spent in the kitchen and turns mealtime into a seamless event. In effect, this creates a nurture-friendly environment for your family, making cooking a source of pleasure rather than pressure.

Your Zero-waste Kitchen also takes care of leftovers,

transforming them into future meals instead of scraps destined for the garbage bin. The key here is to tap into the creativity of cooking and see leftovers as opportunities. Having a set plan enables you to incorporate those leftovers into upcoming meals, becoming an essential part of your menu.

You also contribute to reducing your carbon footprint by consciously avoiding processed and packaged foods. By choosing to cook fresh meals, with portion sizes thought out to prevent waste, you stand against the production and waste of plastics used in packaging. This single change can significantly decrease your personal contribution to landfill masses.

It is also an opportunity to influence healthier diets within the household. Meal prep allows portion control, managing food groups, and ensuring balanced, nutritious intake. It allows for the conscientious integration of diverse food groups into your diet, thus promoting well-rounded nutrition.

In summary, meal planning and smart use of leftovers fit perfectly into the Zero-waste Kitchen model. These not only spur sustainable, eco-friendly living but also foster better health and time management. Not to mention, it's a practical approach that sets you on the path towards contributing to the bigger picture – a sustainable global environment. Your Zero-waste Kitchen could be the first step on your journey to a better world.

Creating a Sustainable Menu

Food preparation in a zero-waste kitchen begins long before you turn on the stove or preheat the oven. It commences with the mindful planning of meal menus towards reducing waste and optimizing resource usage. By adopting a zero-waste approach in meal planning, you're nudging your kitchen practices towards a sustainable and environmentally friendly operation.

Without a doubt, a significant part of this process is keenly planning your meals. Meal planning revolves around designing menus in a way that harnesses the full potential of your ingredients thereby reducing the chances of ending up with unused perishable items that eventually turn into waste. For example, you can plan a series of meals around a particular vegetable or meat to ensure that all parts are utilized, and none goes to waste.

Another central tenet in meal planning is portion control. Monitor and adjust your serving sizes to ensure that all prepared meals are consumed with minimal, and preferably, no leftovers. It's about understanding your family's or your own appetite to consistently prepare the exact quantity of food that will be consumed, hence eliminating waste.

However, sometimes, leftovers are unavoidable. In such instances, embracing a creative approach to repurposing these food remnants plays a pivotal role in the zero-waste endeavor. From crafting new dishes to preserving them properly for future consumption, every leftover has the potential to be transformed and used in entirely innovative ways.

When creating a sustainable menu, consider the environmental footprint of the ingredients you choose. Opt for fresh, locally sourced, and seasonal produce, which not only cuts down on the carbon that thermal refrigeration and long-distance transport inject into the atmosphere but also supports your local economy. Additionally, work towards incorporating more plant-based meals into your routines, as meat and dairy production contribute significantly to greenhouse gases.

Building a zero-waste kitchen is not just about reducing food waste but also about transforming your cooking space into an arena that consciously considers sustainability at every juncture, from planning and preparing meals to handling leftovers and crafting menus. By consciously making these eco-affirmative decisions, your kitchen becomes an agent of change, playing a pivotal role in creating a healthier environment and a sustainable future.

Remember: every dish prepared in a zero-waste kitchen is not just a meal, but a conscious, ethical, and environment-affirmative act that contributes to the global goal of achieving a sustainable future at a micro level.

Maximizing Use of Leftovers

In creating a sustainable, zero-waste kitchen, the preliminary focus should ideally shift towards two pivotal aspects: meal planning and leftovers. By revolutionizing how we approach these norms, we create the foundation for a nourishing, eco-conscious cooking space.

Meal planning is a fundamental step in cutting down waste. We've all been guilty of buying ingredients impulsively, influenced not by necessity, but by fleeting admiration for exotic recipes or seasonal offerings. The result? Wilted greens and spoiled dairy haunting refrigerators and an ever-increasing carbon footprint. By planning meals, we ensure food purchased is food consumed. It's the art of buying what you need, not what you want. Not only does this lessen waste, but it also cultivates healthier eating habits and can prove to be budget friendly.

The paradigm of meal planning hinges on impeccability in determining portions. Understand the nutritional needs of your family. You'll want to consider age, dietary restrictions, health goals, and activity levels. Once you do this, design your meals to meet these requirements, itemizing the ingredients needed. Plan on a weekly basis to start and move to fortnightly or monthly for maximum efficiency.

Now, let's turn our attention to leftovers. Have you ever perceived leftovers as a potential resource rather than remnants of a meal completed? If not, it's time for a sustainable shift in perspective.

Leftovers, when managed correctly, can convert into a treasure trove of meals, markedly reducing waste. But to maximize these leftover benefits, strategic storage is key. Proper storage extends the life and maintains the quality of leftovers, ensuring they remain appetizing. Get creative; labelling helps keep track of when meals were cooked, preventing anything from getting 'lost' in the refrigerator and smoothed over time.

Repurposing leftovers can lead to the discovery of delightful, flavorful combinations. For instance, turning roasted vegetables into savory stews or blending cooked grains into hearty soups are a few of the many possible transformations. It's critical to realize the culinary potential of such surplus food instead of banishing it to the back of the refrigerator.

Pair these practices with eco-friendly cookware and storage options, composting of unavoidable waste, recycling where possible, and sourcing local products, and your zero-waste kitchen will come alive. Such a transformation goes beyond a statement of sustainability. It's an embodiment of a lifestyle that respects the resources it consumes, ensuring we leave the world a healthier and more sustainable place for future generations to thrive.

Storage Solutions for Surplus

In any conscientious kitchen, an eco-minded philosophy is crucial. The aspiration to create a zero-waste kitchen is noble, but also ambitious. However, a potent blend of simple techniques - rooted in meal planning, smart usage, and crafting strategies for leftovers, can all contribute to achieve this objective.

The cornerstone and perhaps the most important step towards minimizing waste in the kitchen revolves around prudent meal planning. Many households suffer from a repetitive pattern of wasted leftover food, and discarded ingredients due to their expiry. By developing a comprehensive meal plan and strictly adhering to it, it becomes easier to purchase the right quantity of ingredients required for the period - which in turn curtails food wastage. Consideration should also be given to methods of cooking and preparation that harness the entire ingredient to minimize waste, such as utilizing vegetable and meat trimmings for stock.

Leftover food presents another challenge, but also an opportunity for innovative solutions to prevent waste. The zero-waste kitchen emphasizes the transformability and reuse of leftovers. Even seemingly unpalatable leftovers can be rebooted into another meal, often times with a simple addition of herbs, spices, or by using them as an ingredient in a whole new dish.

Solutions for surplus management are also integral to a zero-waste kitchen. Sound strategies for dealing with overstock might include not only refrigeration, but also preservation techniques such as canning, pickling, fermenting, and freezing. These techniques can be employed to extend the life of fruits, vegetables, and other perishable food items, preserving their nutritional value and preventing them from heading to landfill.

Storage considerations are significant in a zero-waste kitchen. Traditional plastic storage solutions have hefty ecological footprints; therefore, it is advantageous buying in bulk and adopting sustainable alternatives. Opt for glass, ceramic or stainless-steel containers over their plastic counterparts.

In all these functions, it is clear that creating a zero-waste kitchen necessitates a shift in mindset. But with mindfulness, creativity and planning, you can look forward to transforming your kitchen into a place that respects and values our environment, promotes health and nutrition, and significantly reduces waste. And in doing so, we just might inspire others to follow the same path, amplifying our collective impact on building a more sustainable future.

Reducing Food Prep Waste

Food waste is an alarming and staggeringly prevalent issue, and its rampant prevalence is taking a toll on our environment. However, there is a solution located right in the heart of our homes - the kitchen. Transmuting your ordinary cooking space into a Zero-waste Kitchen not only helps curtail this systemic issue but also brings about a radical change in your lifestyle promoting health, wellbeing, and financial economy.

Food preparation plays a significant role in the transition to a zero-waste kitchen. Thoughtful meal planning is the key first step. By planning your meals in advance, you inherently minimize the opportunity for waste production. When you know the exact ingredients you need, you're less likely to overbuy and consequently, less likely to waste. Not to mention, knowing in advance what you're going to cook gives you the ability to purchase in bulk, reducing the excess packaging that would ordinarily accompany smaller purchases.

Gone are the days when leftovers were simply forgotten in the back of a refrigerator, only to land up in the garbage bin. In a Zero-waste Kitchen, leftovers are a chance to get creative. With mindful meal planning, you can plan for leftovers to be utilized in ways that can boost the nutritional value of subsequent meals. Think stocks from vegetable ends and peels, baked desserts from overripe fruits, or even smoothies with leftover vegetables from your harvest. Interact with your food with respect and no edible food should find its way to your trash bin.

Reducing food prep waste is another pivotal part of the equation. Consciously choosing to purchase unprocessed and packaging free ingredients is a great jump-start. This immediately eliminates the waste generated from food preparation materials such as plastic wrapping, tin foil and container boxes. In lieu of disposable items such as paper towels, utilize reusable items like kitchen towels and rugs. Peelings, ends, pits and stalks (often seen as waste) have culinary potential such as vegetable broths, compost or natural cleaning agents. Even if you need to discard some food scraps, consider composting, a natural way of recycling that converts your waste into a rich supplement for your garden soil.

Transformation isn't achieved in a day. Therefore, don't feel overwhelmed by the prospect of altering your kitchen and food preparation habits. Instead, view this as an ongoing quest towards positive change. The Zero-waste Kitchen isn't a destination, it's a journey. Embrace the process and remember, every effort, however small, counts!

MAINTAINING A ZERO-WASTE KITCHEN

Daily, Weekly, and Monthly Routines

Creating a compost system

The prospect of achieving a zero-waste kitchen may at first seem daunting, especially in our consumption-driven environment. It is, however, an attainable goal that makes use of simple daily, weekly, and monthly routines, as well as efficient waste management systems like composting.

To begin with, daily routines lay the foundation for a zero-waste kitchen. This involves thoughtful, conscious actions such as buying only what is necessary from the grocer's, opting for unpackaged fruits and vegetables, and using reusable shopping bags. Thus, from the point of acquisition, you would have successfully eliminated most sources of kitchen waste.

Similarly, proper food storage is key. Purposefully stocking your refrigerator and pantries can substantially reduce food waste. By storing fruits and vegetables appropriately, their shelf lives are lengthened, reducing occurrences of rotten produce that often ends up in the bin.

The 'Zero-waste' journey also involves cooking practices that minimize waste. Utilizing all parts of a vegetable, for instance, can drastically cut down waste. Perhaps the leaves that usually get discarded could be the hearty addition to a soup, or the peels could be repurposed as zest in a salad. Moreover, portion control while serving meals not only minimizes food waste but also encourages healthy eating habits.

On a weekly level, the concept of 'Zero-waste Meal Prep' becomes instrumental. This involves planning meals around the grocery shopping done and working with what is present in the kitchen before purchasing more items. This sort of intentional cooking significantly reduces waste while saving on grocery bills.

On a monthly level, you would want to perform a kitchen audit. This would involve reviewing your waste, identifying what constitutes the bulk of your waste, and calibrating your shopping, storage, and cooking habits accordingly.

Composting is another fantastic strategy to maintain a zero-waste kitchen. It serves as a natural waste management system, turning kitchen scraps into nutrient-rich soil. Consequently, instead of existing as worthless garbage, your organic waste serves a useful purpose.

Ideally, a successful compost system requires a balance of green waste (e.g., fruit and vegetable scraps, coffee grounds) and brown waste (e.g., dried leaves, cardboard). Turning the compost heap regularly ensures an aerated, efficient composting process, speeding up decay, and minimizing odor.

In conclusion, the idea of having a zero-waste kitchen isn't just about doing away with the plastic or bringing your own shopping bag - it's about fundamentally changing the way we view and interact with food. Achieving such a kitchen revolves around intentional daily, weekly, and monthly habits, coupled with efficient waste management solutions like a compost system. The outcome of these actions is a kitchen space that respects the environment and drastically reduces its ecological footprint.

Implementing sustainable food storage

Implementing a zero-waste kitchen involves a paradigm shift about how you view food, its storage, preparation, and disposal. It absolutely does not call for an overnight change; rather, it's a gradual process that requires strategic planning and a consistent habit-forming mindset. In this light, understanding how to maintain your zero-waste kitchen on a daily, weekly, and monthly basis is vital in the realization of this transformative journey.

On a daily basis, your zero-waste kitchen practice should revolve around sustainable food preparation. This places more emphasis on cooking at home using eco-friendly practices such as menu planning, food batch preparation, and using every part of the ingredient to avoid unnecessary waste.

Furthermore, the use of plastic-free roughage for storing leftovers is a practice that should be incorporated into daily sustainability efforts. Reconsider your traditional storage methods such as switching from plastic wraps and aluminum foils to glass containers or beeswax wraps, which are both reusable and biodegradable.

The practice of composting becomes an imperative daily routine when maintaining a zero-waste kitchen. Any scraps generated through preparation should be composted. It not only reduces the amount of waste directed to the landfill but also improves the fertility of your backyard garden soil.

Week-by-week, this journey requires you to declutter and reassess. There's no need to compromise on aesthetics while aiming for a zero-waste kitchen. Get the right storage items that serve your purpose whilst also embellishing your kitchen space. Another weekly habit to infuse into your routine is to conduct a kitchen inventory. This will keep you abreast of what you already have and prevent unnecessary purchases.

Your shopping routines will also require a much-needed transformation. Move towards purchasing loose or unpackaged goods. Buying in bulk may initially seem daunting but systematically reduces packaging waste and could also save your pennies. Equip yourself with mesh bags, glass jars, or any other sustainable alternatives handy for bulk shopping.

On a monthly basis, cleaning of the kitchen plays a crucial role in its efficiency and the maintenance of a clean and functional workspace. Preferably, use natural homemade cleaners to keep your kitchen surfaces sparkling. These cleaners are cost-effective and also eliminate the need for harsh toxic chemicals detrimental to your health and the environment.

Another monthly task should be to revisit your zero-waste goals. Evaluate the successes and failures. Remember, it's all about forming new habits and such transformations take time, patience, and determination.

Overall, maintaining a zero-waste kitchen isn't another latest eco-trend, it's a lifestyle. More than the intent to transform your kitchen into an eco-friendly haven, it's about making conscious decisions that are beneficial to you, the environment, and future generations.

Utilizing environmentally friendly cleaning products

The concept of maintaining a Zero-waste Kitchen may seem daunting at first glance. However, it can be broken down into simple, achievable daily, weekly, and monthly routines that will not only transform your cooking space into an eco-friendly haven but also create easy habits that become second nature over time.

Daily routines revolve around fundamental decisions and actions. They might be as simple as choosing products packaged in recyclable or compostable materials over those wrapped in plastic or using a cloth bag instead of a single-use one. It also includes developing mindful habits such as planning meals to reduce food waste, storing leftovers correctly to maximize their shelf life, and composting organic waste.

Weekly routines often involve a deeper level of engagement, such as buying in bulk from a local farmers market or a store that allows such an option. Choosing fresh, seasonal produce not only reduces the demand for out-of-season food, which is often shipped over long distances and therefore has a higher carbon footprint, but it also encourages healthier eating habits. Cleaning out the fridge and pantry on a weekly basis ensures that food is consumed before it spoils. All these habits encourage a connection between what we eat and how it affects the world around us.

Monthly routines can include the replacement of non-recyclable or non-compostable items with sustainable alternatives. This can take time, effort, and sometimes an initial investment, but in the long run, such changes can make a significant difference. For instance, replacing disposable kitchen towels with a set of reusable microfiber cloths or switching to energy-efficient appliances when it's time to replace old ones can substantially cut down on waste and energy use.

Cleaning your kitchen with environmentally friendly products that have been certified as safe for the planet is another crucial aspect of leading a zero-waste lifestyle. Conventional cleaning products can often contain harsh chemicals that can harm the environment as well as our health. In contrast, sustainable cleaning products use biodegradable components and come in packaging that can be reused or recycled.

The journey towards a Zero-waste Kitchen requires a paradigm shift and a commitment to sustainability. It necessitates us to pause, evaluate, and reflect on our choices and actions. This shift transcends big sweeping changes and instead focuses on the power of small, mindful choices and habits that add up to substantial positive changes for the world. Together, we can make the transition to a sustainable, zero-waste lifestyle, starting with our kitchens.

Organizing waste separation habits

Creating, maintaining, and enhancing a zero-waste kitchen is a process that invariably involves meticulous planning, unwavering commitment, and persistent implementation. These elements intertwine with your daily, weekly, and monthly routines to bring to life the concept of a kitchen that not only overflows with culinary charm but also integrates eco-friendly habits seamlessly into the essence of its existence.

In your daily routine, you would ideally start by re-evaluating your cooking style. The initial step is to consciously reduce the amount of waste produced through meal preparation. Instead of pre-packaged goods, consider buying loose produce, which instantly eliminates a chunk of your plastic waste. Find a home composting system that works for you and start composting organic waste daily at home. Each day, set aside some time to wash and sort recyclable materials such as glass, cans, and certain types of plastic. Make this a joy rather than a chore, incorporating it into your regular kitchen clean-up routine.

On a weekly basis, planning your meals is crucial to minimizing unnecessary waste. When you know what you are going to eat on each day of the week, you'll only purchase what you need, reducing potential food wastage considerably and ensuring that everything you buy is used effectively. Take an extra step by choosing to shop at stores or markets that favor organic and locally grown produce. Not only does it reduce the carbon footprint associated with transport, but it also supports local farmers. By the end of each week, assess the waste produced and identify areas where improvements can be made.

Your monthly habits should focus on a broader scope, involving community engagement and schedule adherence. Engage in monthly swaps or donations of non-perishable food items with your neighbors. It's a great way to ensure items get used before they expire while fostering community relationships. Committed adherence to your waste segregation and recycling schedule is imperative on a monthly basis as well.

Finally, maintaining a Zero-waste Kitchen is contingent upon how effectively you integrate waste separation habits into the aforementioned routines. As the lynchpin of your waste-minimization efforts, waste separation should be treated as a non-negotiable part of your cleaning routine. This practice involves separating organic waste from recyclables and non-recyclables, as well as understanding what local recycling facilities accept. This effort, consistently applied, will not merely transform your kitchen into a hub of sustainability but also kindle a broader awareness in your lifestyle, gradually guiding you to tread lightly on the world that sustains us.

In essence, a zero-waste kitchen is an achievable objective that demands heightened consciousness, mindful practices, and committed consistency. As you embark on this journey, remember that curiosity and patience are your friends, and each small step is a significant stride towards creating a haven that both you, and the Earth, can be proud of. Your evolving eco-friendly sanctuary awaits you, filled with the promise of transformation that far exceeds its physical boundaries.

Initiating effective reuse techniques

In a world riddled with pollution and waste, the concept of a zero-waste kitchen is as appealing as it is necessary. By transforming your cooking space into an eco-friendly haven, you significantly cut back on waste, reduce your carbon footprint, and promote a healthier environment for future generations.

To maintain a zero-waste kitchen, daily, weekly, and monthly routines are essential. While change might seem overwhelming at first, through steady consistency and ritual reinforcement, the move towards a waste-free kitchen becomes easier and more efficient.

On a daily basis, mindful consumption needs to be at the forefront. This involves rethinking your food choices. Opt for foods with less packaging or buy in bulk where possible. This makes a huge difference in waste reduction. Items such as rice, pasta, grains, and beans can be bought in bulk, stored in reusable containers, and cut down on waste significantly.

After every meal, recycle what can't be avoided. Food scraps, such as vegetable peels and fruit rinds, are perfect for compost. This compost, when designated in a backyard bin or collection service, can then be returned to the soil to nourish plants and gardens. The daily practice of composting also greatly reduces the amount of organic waste that usually ends up in landfills.

Weekly routines should focus on meal planning and shopping. Taking the time each week to properly plan your meals eliminates last-minute purchases and avoids unnecessary food waste. When grocery shopping, bring your own reusable bags, containers, and mesh produce bags to avoid single-use plastics. Consider visiting farmer's markets or local farm shops where fresh produce often comes with less packaging and helps support the local farming community.

On a monthly basis, one could do a regular audit of pantry stocks and fridge content. This not only helps with meal planning but also aids in identifying problem areas and food items that consistently contribute to waste. From here, you can make informed decisions on replacements or alternatives that are more environmentally friendly.

Embarking upon a zero-waste kitchen journey also calls for effective reuse techniques. Glass jars from pasta sauces or pickles can act as perfect storage containers for bulk dry goods, spices or leftovers. Old newspapers can be used for lining compost bins, while vegetable scraps can be stored in the freezer for future veggie broths.

Investing in quality, long-lasting kitchen equipment that will stand the test of time is another crucial aspect of an eco-friendly kitchen. Rather than using disposable kitchen towels, switch to cloth towels that can be washed and reused. Silicone baking mats can replace parchment paper, and beeswax wraps are an excellent alternative to plastic cling wrap.

Promoting a zero-waste kitchen does not mean achieving absolute perfection at all times. It is about undertaking consistent actions, investing in sustainable practices, and manifesting value in preservation over waste. With time, these efforts compound into habits that not only benefit the environment but also create an organized, efficient, and mindful cooking space. Implementing these routines propels us further towards our goal - a haven of kitchen sustainability where nothing is wasted, and everything has a purpose and place.

Challenges and their Solutions

Overcoming food waste

Keeping the sanctity of a kitchen signifies much more than just maintaining its cleanliness. Today, as environmental concerns gain ground, sustainability has become the focal point of discussions making 'Zero-waste Kitchen' a trending topic. This engaging concept promotes mitigating waste production in the kitchen and advocates for sustainable and conscious living.

However, achieving the concept of a zero-waste kitchen is not without its challenges. The most pressing of these lies in the management of food waste. Each year in the US alone, roughly 30%-40% of the total food supply gets wasted. Quite astonishingly, each of us has a significant role to play in this irreversible loss, and our kitchens are the theatres where much of this drama of destruction unfolds.

Overcoming these challenges may seem formidable on the surface, but armed with the right knowledge and approach, it becomes not only feasible but an empowering journey. Here we delineate the root causes of these challenges, their repercussions, and the actionable strategies to overcome them.

A major cause of food waste is the lack of proper planning. When we do not plan our meals and grocery shopping effectively, we tend to overbuy, leading to overstocking and ultimately waste. Ensuring only the necessary quantities are purchased and consumed can drastically cut down waste.

Another issue lies in the improper storage of food. Many times, perishable food items are improperly stored leading to spoilage. Adopting correct preservation techniques, understanding the shelf-life of different food products, and efficient management of refrigerator and pantry spaces will promote sustainable practices.

Rescuing leftovers also falls under effective food management. These neglected pieces of food are often thrown away, creating waste when they can be creatively used in other recipes or composted.

Meticulous segregation of waste forms another pivotal part of managing a zero-waste kitchen. Dividing waste into recyclable, compostable, and non-compostable can significantly reduce the overall waste that goes into landfills.

Cultivating sustainable habits does not happen overnight, it is a gradual process. The key is persistently practicing these strategies until they become second nature. Remember, every small step counts in achieving a larger goal. The rewards we reap in the form of an eco-friendly environment and conscious living are beyond measuring in material terms.

The journey of maintaining a zero-waste kitchen requires a shift in mindset and a commitment to adapt to new, greener ways. It isn't just a lifestyle change, but a responsible choice for the environment and a sustainable future. Let's embrace this transformative journey, one kitchen at a time.

Efficient storage solutions

Creating and maintaining a zero-waste kitchen indeed presents challenges, some of which may appear insurmountable. The thought of completely eliminating food waste and maintaining a perfectly environmentally friendly kitchen may be overwhelming, given the fact that many kitchen products and foods come in multiple layers of wasteful packaging, and that many food scraps are often just thrown into the trash.

However, by addressing these challenges systematically and implementing thoughtful solutions, it is entirely possible to turn your kitchen into a zero-waste haven.

One of the most prevalent challenges is food packaging waste. All too often, our groceries are packaged in plastic film, containers, and other non-reusable material. Out of convenience, we throw them away, adding to landfill waste. To overcome this hurdle, opt for products with minimal to no packaging where possible. Invest in reusable grocery bags, consider shopping at farmer's markets, food cooperatives, or other stores that offer bulk items and allow you to bring your own containers.

Food waste from leftover meals or spoiling food is another high impact area. Fortunately, there are several efficient strategies to address this problem. Meal planning and sticking to a grocery list can greatly reduce the amount of extra food that ends up spoiling and being tossed out. Preserving excess food through canning, freezing, and fermenting are also useful methods to stretch your food's lifespan. Composting kitchen scraps is another solution that not only reduces waste but enriches your garden soil.

Storage solutions play an essential role in creating an efficient, zero-waste kitchen. Disorganization leads to forgotten food items that spoil, repeated purchases of the same item, and a stressful kitchen environment. Clear, stackable storage containers can help keep your pantry tidy and food items visible. You can repurpose glass jars from purchased food items (e.g., pickles, sauces) as storage containers - a zero-waste win-win.

By choosing to refill your used glass or stainless steel containers instead of buying another plastic-wrapped packet, maintaining a streamlined pantry to better monitor food conditions and expiration dates, and embracing composting, you are embarking on a transformative process. With resolve, education, and small sequential changes, turning your cooking space into an eco-friendly haven is an attainable goal.

Sustainable shopping habits

Modernizing our lifestyles to prioritize environmental sustainability can be challenging, but it is a rewarding initiative. One of the major spaces we can focus on transformation is the kitchen. Efficiently managing kitchen activities while adhering to zero-waste principles requires commitment and strategic planning. This section aims to furnish you with practical strategies to help you maintain a zero-waste kitchen and overcome potential issues while fostering sustainable shopping habits.

Firstly, understanding that a zero-waste kitchen isn't achieved overnight but rather a series of conscious better choices and changes is crucial. It requires a shift from the 'use and dispose of' mindset to a more sustainable 'reuse and recycle' mentality. Pursuing a sustainable kitchen means making the most of leftovers, minimizing food wastage, eliminating single-use goods, and being deliberate about shopping methods.

In dealing with the challenge of grocery packaging, for instance, sources like farmers' markets or bulk-buy stores are laudable alternatives. These allow for the purchase of fresh, package-free produce, or in larger quantities to minimize packaging needs. Carrying personal, reusable bags, jars, or containers during grocery shopping can also curb the use of plastic bags and unnecessary packaging.

Tools like a compost bin or a worm farm can be handy in terms of organic waste. Instead of tossing vegetable peels, coffee grounds, or eggshells into the trash, these can be composted and used as nutrient-rich soil for plants. This means fewer non-biodegradable bags are filled and there's less waste going to the landfill.

While kitchen appliances and gadgets can aid in preparing meals efficiently, investing in durable, versatile, and energy-efficient ones combat the commercial cycle of 'buy-use-discard'. Repairing rather than replacing is another sustainable practice worth mentioning here.

Food storage is another crucial aspect of a zero-waste kitchen. Reusable silicone bags, glass jars, cloth wraps, and stainless steel canisters are just some of the options available. These solutions not only reduce the use of plastic wraps and bags but also keep food fresher for longer.

Managing food wastage, another giant in the race towards a zero-waste kitchen, can be solved by careful meal planning and organization. Regularly checking the items in the refrigerator and pantry and prioritizing the use of ingredients near their expiry dates, or using a 'first in, first out' system can limit waste.

In sum, the road to a zero-waste kitchen might be filled with hurdles; however, it is an inspiring endeavor that promises immense rewards. The issues posed may seem overwhelming at first but focusing on one change at a time can lead to a substantial and productive shift, edging us closer to our ultimate ecological obligation - a cleaner and more sustainable environment.

Recycling kitchen by-products

Maintaining a zero-waste kitchen is an ambitious but attainable goal, one that many aspire to reach as part of their commitment to environmental stewardship. The process, however, can bring its share of challenges. Confronting these obstacles with well-thought solutions could potentially establish a pathway towards a more sustainable way of cooking and living.

One of the main hurdles you may encounter when transitioning to a zero-waste kitchen is the ingrained habit of using disposable items. Many people typically use and discard items daily such as plastic utensils, paper towels, and packaging materials. This reliance is a significant contributor to the ever-growing global waste problem. Fortunately, there is a straightforward solution. Embrace reusable alternatives such as cloth napkins, stainless steel utensils, and glass storage containers.

When shopping, another common issue arises: the pervasiveness of plastic packaging in the retail sector. Meat, fruits, vegetables, and grocery items are often swathed in plastic wrap or contained in plastic bags or containers, contributing greatly to plastic pollution. A possible workaround here is to take keener interest and responsibility in how we procure our food. Consider visiting local farmer's markets where you could bring your containers, or support refill stores and zero-waste shops where you bring your clean, reusable containers to be refilled with staple goods, thereby eliminating waste.

Food waste is yet another adversary in the race towards a zero-waste kitchen. Leftovers and food spoilage are the leading types of kitchen waste, but they can be mitigated by attentive meal planning, better storage methods, and composting. Meal planning is a solution that will allow you to buy what you need, thus reducing the likelihood of leftovers or spoilage. Simple practices such as storing food in clear containers so you see what's inside, or arranging your refrigerator in the order of oldest to newest can greatly reduce food waste. For unavoidable waste like fruit peels and vegetable scraps, maintaining a compost pile at home can convert these organic wastes into a rich soil supplement.

Lastly, recycling is a crucial part of maintaining a zero-waste kitchen, but knowing what can be recycled and how to recycle them properly can be confusing. Having a proper segregation system in your kitchen can certainly make the process less daunting. Understanding and following your local recycling guidelines and visiting recycling centers can help sustain our commitment towards a zero-waste kitchen.

In conclusion, the challenges of maintaining a zero-waste kitchen are real but not insurmountable. It is a lifestyle switch that revolves around conscious choices, discipline, and a genuine commitment to our planet's health. It's about respect for resources, opting for reusables, eliminating unnecessary waste, composting, and recycling, but most importantly, it's about being a responsible inhabitant of this one world we share and cherish. Remember, every small step towards a zero-waste kitchen makes a profound impact in our collective sustainability efforts.

Rethinking kitchen design

Maintaining a zero-waste kitchen is not merely a trend; it is rather an essential lifestyle alteration that can significantly contribute to a more sustainable and environment-friendly living. This engages in reducing waste, reusing resources, and recycling materials to attain a lean and green kitchen environment. However, transitioning to a zero-waste kitchen comes with its own set of challenges. Even so, remember, each challenge is a beckoning opportunity for growth and innovation.

The first challenge that may seem daunting is the sheer amount of waste generated by a regular kitchen. Plastics, packaging materials, uneaten food, and wasted water contribute to a majority of kitchen waste. These materials often end up in landfills or the ocean, contributing to pollution and harming the environment.

However, steps can be taken to cut down on this waste drastically. Start by considering the materials that you purchase. Opt for bulk-buying food items from local farmers markets to reduce unnecessary packaging waste. Switch to sustainable materials and practices-such as glass over plastic. Consider composting as a method to reuse kitchen- and garden-related waste, which eventually can be converted into nutrient-rich soil for plants.

The second challenge arises from the conventional kitchen design—foreseen to be a repository of packaged goods, non-reusable containers, and electronic appliances. The task here is to reimagine and redesign your kitchen so it is in harmony with zero-waste principles.

One could primarily start by decluttering the kitchen space, removing non-reusable and non-recyclable items, and replacing them with eco-friendly alternatives. Use glass jars for storage, returnable milk bottles, and compostable dish brushes. Also, consider energy-efficient appliances, which help cut down substantially on electricity usage.

Water wastage is another sobering aspect in kitchen design. Simple steps such as fixing leaks timely, using aerators on faucets, and repurposing water from rinsing fruits and vegetables can conserve a significant amount of water.

Lastly, the process can seem overwhelming and time-consuming. However, remember that transitioning to a zero-waste kitchen is not an overnight change. The essence of it lies in the gradual implementation of eco-friendly practices and the consistent adaptation of resourceful habits.

Be patient with yourself throughout this process; every effort you make, no matter how small, brings us closer to a more sustainable and eco-friendlier world. By keeping these strategies in mind, turning your kitchen into a zero-waste haven is an entirely achievable and rewarding goal.

Involving Family Members

Establish shared responsibility

As we embark on this journey toward creating a zero-waste kitchen, it is important to recognize that waste is not just an individual problem; it is a communal issue. Achieving a zero-waste kitchen is not a task for one person alone, but an initiative that should engage every member of the household, making it a team effort rooted in the commitment to sustainability.

Engaging family members in maintaining a zero-waste kitchen can be beneficial in multiple ways. Not only is it a tangible way to involve everyone in the eco-friendly endeavor, but it also provides an opportunity to educate each other about the impacts of waste on our environment and instill responsible habits that can have a ripple effect beyond the confines of the kitchen.

Firstly, communication is key. We need to clearly explain to our family members why we are making these changes and what benefits they can bring. This can be an opportunity to impart knowledge about environmental issues, the problem of waste overproduction and how it impacts our world. Providing this context can help family members view the changes not as a burden, but as a necessary contribution toward a larger, global goal.

To establish shared responsibility, it can be useful to assign different tasks to different family members according to their strengths and interests. Maybe one person is responsible for meal planning to minimize food waste; another takes charge of composting kitchen scraps; someone else could be in charge of ensuring that recyclables are properly disposed of. Dividing tasks this way not only lessens the load for one person, but it also gives everyone a sense of ownership of the mission.

In order to motivate and encourage participation, setting collective goals can be beneficial. Tracking progress together, celebrating achievements and small victories can provide a sense of collaboration and encourage continued commitment. Maybe a reward system might spark the interest of the younger members of the household.

Involving family members in this initiative serves a dual purpose. We create an eco-friendly kitchen and at the same time instill a sense of responsibility in our family members. This is an investment in our future; as we teach these principles to our children, we raise a generation of conscious, ecologically responsible citizens who will carry these habits with them for life. Remember, the goal of achieving a zero-waste kitchen doesn't require perfection, instead, it advocates for the consistent and conscious effort in reducing waste and caring for our environment.

Promote eco-friendly practices

The mandate of maintaining a zero-waste kitchen is inextricably tied to the ethos of sustainability, preservation, and caretaking for our planet. By persistently embracing and purposefully integrating zero-waste practices into your cooking space, you can create an impressive, lasting impact on the environment, unwittingly becoming a beacon for others to follow.

Your kitchen, often the heart of a home, is central to making this change effective. It is the space that generates the most waste and therefore can deliver the highest impact through transformation. However, it isn't just about your commitment to change, but equally about involving all family members in this process of transformation. Remember, the journey to creating an eco-friendly haven is not a solitary one. It is a shared striving, a collective effort.

Begin with open and enlightening discussions about the importance of decreasing waste and the collective benefits it can bring to the earth and future generations. Educate them about the role of a single consumer in the larger environmental picture. Encourage questions, inspire curiosity and foster a spirit of responsible consumption. Lead by example, showcasing how easily discarded items like vegetable peelings can be composted or plastic containers converted into storage devices.

Inculcate a culture of mindful consumerism in your family. Encourage your family members to think about the life cycle of any product before purchasing it: from its creation, use, and finally, to its disposal. Cultivate a practice of purchasing items that are durable, repairable, and recyclable. Make them understand the significance of rejecting over-packaged goods and choosing to buy in bulk to cut down on waste.

Promoting eco-friendly practices is also key in maintaining a zero-waste kitchen. Experiment with creative ways to repurpose or reuse items before considering disposal. Compost organic waste to use as rich soil for your home garden, thereby closing the loop of food consumption. Practical elements such as energy-efficient appliances, low-flow kitchen faucets, or LED lighting can also contribute substantially to an eco-friendly kitchen.

Also, make practical commitments as a family to waste reduction goals and regularly gauge your progress. Be patient as implementing new routines and habits takes time. Celebrate small victories together and motivate each other in weak moments.

The quantum leap from a regular to a zero-waste kitchen might seem intimidating but remember, every tiny step counts. A solitary action can catalyze widespread change. By transforming your kitchen into an eco-friendly haven, you are not just reforming your lifestyle; you are part of a global movement towards environmental conservation, setting a precious example for younger generations to emulate.

Implement waste segregation

Creating and maintaining a zero-waste kitchen is a challenging yet fulfilling endeavor that requires consistent efforts, mindful alterations, and the involvement of everyone under the same roof. This chapter discusses the concept of zero-waste, the importance of family participation, and the constructive approach of waste segregation in cultivating an eco-friendly environment within the confines of your kitchen.

The zero-waste kitchen movement represents a sweeping change in habits, lifestyle, and perspective. It calls for a radical shift from the throw-away society to an ecosystem where every item has its place and purpose. It's about minimizing waste, nurturing creative reuse, and sweating the small stuff, literally. But the magic of zero-waste kitchen unfolds only when it's a collective effort.

Involving family members in the process isn't just about sharing workloads; it's about fostering an inclusive environment where everyone appreciates and contributes to the common goal. It involves education, discussion, and even some level of negotiation at times. But the success of a zero-waste kitchen lies in making every family member a stakeholder, a participant with an equal sense of responsibility and commitment.

Guiding the family to embrace habits such as cloth shopping bags instead of plastics, refillable water bottles instead of single-use, and compostable dishes and cutlery instead of disposables is critical. Also crucial is introducing waste segregation, which soon becomes a standard protocol in the household and assists in achieving the target of a zero-waste kitchen.

Waste segregation is the frontline defense against waste. It's a practice where waste is separated based on type, ensuring it's headed in the right direction whether that means reuse, recycling or decomposing. Waste segregation in a kitchen involves separate bins for dry and wet waste - dry waste includes items like cardboard packaging and glass bottles, wet waste includes vegetable peels and other organic matter which can be composted.

Zero-waste in a kitchen doesn't mean achieving absolute zero but to persistently aiming for it via practice and patience. To incorporate waste segregation, preferencing reusable items, and involving the family in maintaining a green kitchen, signifies a significant step in the right direction. With a comprehensive understanding and solid execution of these practices, transforming your cooking space into an eco-friendly haven doesn't remain an ambitious dream but an attainable reality.

Creating and maintaining a zero-waste kitchen is a daily pilgrimage towards an environment-friendly lifestyle. It demonstrates, in no uncertain terms, that it's feasible and desirable to distance ourselves from a throw-away culture and inch closer to a sustainable future. This move might appear to be small, but its impact is broad and wide - influencing not just you and your loved ones, but also inspiring far-reaching ripples of sustainable practices and mindsets beyond your kitchen walls.

Encourage sustainable shopping habits

The Zero-waste Kitchen is not a concept that manifests overnight. It's a journey that involves education, adjustment of habits, and most crucially, the involvement of the whole family unit. Maintaining a Zero-waste Kitchen is a concerted team effort, predicated on the understanding and adoption of sustainable practices by all family members.

To foster this integration, patience and open communication are key. Engage in frequent conversations about the importance of sustainability – why it matters and how it helps. By breaking down the cause and effects, each individual gains an understanding of their role within this wider context. Encourage each member to share their ideas and thoughts on how to contribute to and further evolve these practices.

Heeded and empowered by knowledge, family members will naturally find it easier to modify actions and behaviors that are contrary to this lifestyle. Remember to appreciate these changes, no matter how small they may initially seem. Celebrating victories together as a family fortifies the commitment to this shared goal.

Sustainable shopping habits are a pillar of the Zero-waste Kitchen. To ensure success, structure your shopping process around three broad stages – preparation, purchasing, and post-purchase management.

Preparation involves comprehensive meal planning. By knowing exactly what to buy, you avoid unnecessary purchases that often contribute to food waste. This foresight also implores a list-making habit that not only streamlines your shopping experience but also reduces the risk of impulse buying.

The purchasing stage requires conscious selection. Choose local, seasonal produce over imported varieties. This decision not only reduces your carbon footprint but also supports local economies. Where possible, buy in bulk. Bulk purchasing eliminates the need for individual packaging for each item, significantly reducing the amount of waste you bring into your kitchen.

Post-purchase management focuses on the efficient use and storage of your produce to minimize waste. This includes understanding and implementing proper food storage techniques to extend shelf life and experimenting with creative recipes to use up leftovers.

Remember, a Zero-waste Kitchen does not demand perfection. It seeks progress. By continuously learning, instilling, and refining sustainable practices, your kitchen will gradually and inevitably transform into an eco-friendly haven, inspiring others in its wake.

Foster creativity in leftovers

In today's rapidly changing world where convenience reigns supreme, transforming our cooking space into a zero-waste kitchen can be a task riddled with difficulty. However, adopting a zero-waste lifestyle doesn't entail a drastic or immediate change. It is a process, a journey of slowly implementing sustainable practices in your kitchen.

Maintaining a zero-waste kitchen is a holistic endeavor, where each member of the family contributes. It promotes responsibility towards the environment and can be a transformative experience. The prospect of getting your family members involved in this initiative can be tackled in many creative and engaging ways.

Education is the cornerstone of any new implementation. Begin by instilling an understanding of the zero-waste concept. Discuss the implications of food wastage and the environmental impact it carries. Make it a family goal, setting milestones and rewards to encourage everyone's participation.

Grocery-shopping habits play a crucial role in waste generation. As a family, make a commitment to purchase in bulk, avoiding packaged products, thereby reducing plastic consumption. This could be further enhanced by growing your own herbs and vegetables.

Creating a zero-waste kitchen also calls for a change in food preparation techniques. Invest in durable kitchen tools that last longer than disposable ones. Encourage members to use all parts of a vegetable or meat while cooking. Composting kitchen waste is an excellent practice that reinforces the zero-waste principles.

Leftovers often find their way to the garbage bin. But in a zero-waste kitchen, they must be seen as a treasure of culinary potential. Encourage your family members to explore creative ways to incorporate leftovers into the next meal. This will not only reduce wastage but also foster a culture of innovation and creativity in your home. From creating a one-pot casserole dish with leftover vegetables to using yesterday's chicken in a homemade savory pie, the opportunities are limitless.

Remember, a zero-waste kitchen is constantly evolving. Patience, persistence, and creativity are key to maintain and continually develop this sustainable space. It is a collective effort, one that promises rewarding results for your family and the environment.

DEALING WITH WASTE IN A ZERO-WASTE KITCHEN

Understanding Composting

Basics of kitchen composting

In striving towards cultivating a zero-waste kitchen, we must effectively address the manner in which waste is handled. Reducing kitchen waste to zero may seem like an impossible endeavor; however, it mainly involves re-thinking our habits, making the most of our ingredients and learning how to dispose of inevitable waste in an environmentally friendly manner. One key practice in achieving this aspiration is composting - a process that transforms organic waste into nutrient-rich soil.

Composting is an eco-friendly method of waste disposal that not only diminishes the amount of trash produced in the kitchen but also contributes positively towards soil enhancement. A well-managed compost bin eliminates the need for artificial fertilizers, as it provides an organic, nutrient-rich additive for garden soils. Composting contributes to a sustainable lifestyle by re-utilizing waste, reducing landfill contribution and cultivating healthier soils.

Understanding composting is integral to adopting this beneficial practice. Kitchen waste such as vegetable scraps, coffee grounds, eggshells, and other non-meat, non-dairy organic material can be used as the base for compost. Central to the composting process is the balance of "green" materials - which are high in nitrogen, and "brown" materials - which are rich in carbon. Green materials can include fruit and vegetable waste, coffee grounds, and fresh grass clippings. Conversely, brown materials can include dry leaves, paper, straw, or wood chips.

When considering starting a kitchen compost bin, small countertop containers or larger outdoor bins may be used, depending on individual needs and available space. Each presents a viable means of storing compostable material until it can be moved to a more permanent composting location, such as a heap in the backyard or a local composting facility.

It's important to note that not all food waste is compostable. Meat, dairy products, diseased plants, and chemically treated wood products should be excluded. These materials either attract pests, create unpleasant odors or introduce harmful substances to your compost.

In conclusion, composting is an essential part of the zero-waste kitchen. It's a process that calls for a slight learning curb, but its positive impact on the environment makes it a worthy endeavor. By rethinking our waste habits and using resources wisely, we can elevate our kitchens from being mere cooking spaces to being environmentally responsible havens. Composting's value is twofold: it ensures waste reduction while also enhancing the growth of new life in our gardens and farms. The zero-waste kitchen is achievable, and composting is an essential step on the path towards it.

Composting options: indoors vs outdoors

Cultivating a zero-waste kitchen necessitates a radical rethinking of our relationship with food, from purchase to disposal. The concept isn't just about recycling or obsessing over a tiny garbage can, instead, it's about essentially restructuring our culinary practices to reduce, reuse, and respect our resources.

In the world of zero-waste, one technique stands out as a remarkably effective tool to manage organic waste - composting. Composting, in simplest terms, is a natural process where organic materials like kitchen scraps decompose into a rich soil conditioner, commonly known as compost. It is not only an excellent technique for reducing kitchen waste but is also incredibly beneficial for the soil in our garden, turning our waste into worth.

Dealing with waste in a zero-waste kitchen means comprehending the full life cycle of each ingredient and understanding the potential uses of every part, especially when it comes to organic waste. Composting offers the dual benefit of reducing landfill-bound waste while simultaneously enriching our soil.

Understanding composting really comes down to one basic principle: Biological decomposition. The process is facilitated by a legion of microorganisms, turning your scraps into an excellent, almost free, source of nutrients for your plants. It might seem complicated at a glance, but once understood, composting becomes a natural part of a zero-waste kitchen lifestyle.

When it comes to actual composting, one always has the option of either going outdoors or indoors. Your composting strategy will depend on several factors but primarily it hinges upon your available space and the volume of waste that you generate.

Outdoor composting might require a larger dedicated space in your backyard, where you place organic waste in a pile or enclosed in a box or drum. For a successful outdoor compost, maintaining moisture levels, a proper ratio of green to brown waste and regular turning for aeration is essential. While it might need some manual labor, it is an easy, economical, and efficient means of composting large volumes of waste.

Indoor composting, on the other hand, is great for those living in apartments or homes without adequate outdoor space. Typically, indoor composting makes use of a designated bin and specific types of waste, such as fruit and vegetable peels, coffee grounds, and eggshells. Many indoor techniques, like worm composting or bokashi, are odorless and require less space, offering a manageable composting solution regardless of your living situation.

In conclusion, composting is a pivotal aspect of the zero-waste kitchen ideal. It offers a way to return the nutrients back to the earth, nurturing the very ground that provides us sustenance, echoing the circular economy principle of a zero-waste lifestyle. Understanding composting and your options with regard to it might necessitate a shift in perspective, but with commitment, it becomes an integral part of your eco-friendly kitchen and household.

Choosing appropriate compost container

Dealing with waste is an inevitable part of kitchen activities, especially when attempting to create a sustainable, eco-friendly kitchen. Approaching this challenge proactively and creatively may lead to the establishment of a zero-waste kitchen, fundamentally revolutionizing the cooking space into an earth-friendly haven. At the heart of this sustainable transformation lies the practical, yet often overlooked, technique of composting.

Composting refers to the process of decomposing organic kitchen waste - from fruit peels and vegetable cuttings to coffee grounds and eggshells - into nutrient-rich soil, also known as compost. This natural resource serves multiple purposes such as enriching garden soils, reducing the need for chemical fertilizers, and most importantly, aiding the significant reduction of landfill-bound household waste. It is a win-win solution that connects your kitchen to nature while minimizing environmental impact.

Establishing an effective composting system in your kitchen involves several critical factors, one of which is choosing the most suitable compost container. It is a decision that should be based on your available space, the layout of your kitchen, and your personal preferences regarding aesthetics and functionality.

For those with ample outdoor space, consider setting up a compost bin or a compost pile in your backyard. This approach allows for the composting of large amounts of kitchen waste, as well as yard waste like leaves or grass clippings. However, it might require more labor in terms of mixing and turning the compost material.

For those living in apartments or homes with limited outdoor spaces, indoor compost bins can be the ideal solution. These containers are typically compact, odor-free, and easy to maintain. They are designed in a wide variety of styles ranging from plastic containers with lids to stainless steel bins with charcoal filters, allowing homeowners to choose one that aligns with their kitchen's design.

Ultimately, the journey towards a zero-waste kitchen requires patience, innovation, and a commitment towards sustainability. Embracing composting as an essential part of this journey, coupled with choosing the appropriate compost container, paves the way for a significant transformation of your kitchen into a space that respects and nourishes the environment while offering a healthier lifestyle for you and your family. It is a journey where every step counts, and every decision holds the potential to make a huge environmental difference.

Composting: what to include

One of the fundamental elements in advocating a Zero-waste Kitchen is dealing effectively with waste. In a traditional cooking space, considerable amounts of food scraps, peels, and leftovers often end up in landfills, contributing to significant environmental harm through the release of methane - a potent greenhouse gas. The Zero-waste Kitchen approach reimagines this failure into opportunity, with strategies to reduce, repurpose, recycle and regenerate. Perhaps the most potent of these is composting.

Composting is a natural process that converts organic waste into rich, nutrient-filled humus, the life-giving layer of soil that contributes to plant growth. In the context of an eco-friendly kitchen, it implies the repurposing of biodegradable waste - those kitchen scraps traditionally sent thoughtlessly to landfills - into a resource beneficial for the environment. A brilliant and practical solution that diminishes waste, it lowers your carbon footprint while simultaneously enriching your home garden or pot plants.

At this point the typical question emerges, 'what can be composted?' The answer includes the unexpected, a treasure trove of materials often discarded without a second thought. Vegetable and fruit peelings, coffee grounds, tea bags, plant trimmings, leaves, grass clippings - all are ideal for compost. Likewise, paper materials, from shredded newspaper to paper towels and bags, are excellent additions. Composting is undeniably versatile.

Eggshells, while surprising, are also desirable inclusions. Crushed eggshells add useful minerals to your compost, particularly calcium, an essential plant nutrient. Remember to crush them into tiny pieces to hasten their decomposition.

Several materials, however, should be avoided in your compost heap. These include meat, dairy products, diseased plants, and pet waste, amongst others. Such materials attract pests, can create unpleasant odors, and can spread disease.

Finally, remember that composting is not merely an act of waste reduction; it's a lifestyle change that mirrors the cyclical beauty of life. From life to death to rebirth, composting illustrates a continuous cycle of renewal. Embracing composting within your kitchen aids in the larger struggle to protect and sustain our shared home, the Earth.

Switching to a Zero-waste Kitchen may appear daunting initially. Dealing with waste and understanding composting are new to many. However, the transition can be smooth if initiated mindfully and with patience, and the rewards are myriad – for you, your wallet, your garden, and strikingly, the world around you. Composting is a vital tool in your Zero-waste repertoire, helping inch the world closer to a more sustainable, eco-friendly future.

Maintaining a healthy compost pile

In the journey towards crafting a zero-waste kitchen, managing the waste, correctly and efficiently, becomes one of the priority areas of focus. When it comes to a sustainable lifestyle, it's about adopting strategies that reduce waste to a minimum, and composting, indeed, is a practice that should be integrated into our daily habits.

Composting is the natural process in which organic material decomposes under the optimal conditions into a nutrient-rich substance known as compost. This process plays an integral part in reducing kitchen waste and significantly contributing to the health of the environment. It keeps a substantial amount of kitchen waste out of landfills, reducing methane gas production which contributes to global warming. Furthermore, it also encourages the production of beneficial bacteria and fungi that break down organic matter to create humus, a nutrient-rich material that enhances soil fertility and stimulates healthy plant growth when used as a soil conditioner.

The raw materials for composting can be found easily within our kitchens. They include coffee grounds, eggshells, vegetable and fruit peels, tea bags, among other organic waste items. Combining these materials, termed as 'greens' with 'browns' such as dried leaves, small branches or shredded newspapers, leads to the creation of a balanced compost pile.

Maintaining a healthy compost pile requires specific knowledge and care. It's not a simple process of throwing waste into a bin and forgetting about it. For composting to be successful, it requires the right balance of 'greens' and 'browns' mentioned earlier. Greens provide nitrogen and are quick to decompose, while browns offer carbon and decompose slower, providing a steady supply of fresh material to compost. A healthy compost pile should have a balance, ideally a 3:1 ratio of browns to greens.

In addition to maintaining the right components, proper aeration and moisture levels are vital. A well-aerated compost pile promotes breakdown by aerobic bacteria, speeding up the process. Therefore, turning your compost pile regularly is recommended. Moisture acts as a catalyst for the breaking down process, so the pile must be kept damp but not overly wet.

Understanding the science behind composting, along with its benefits, can profoundly impact our approach towards waste management in our kitchens. It aids us in achieving the goal of crafting a zero-waste kitchen, paving the road to a more sustainable lifestyle. Remember, every step counts when it comes to environmental sustainability. Even our smallest actions can make a difference. Embracing composting in our everyday lives is undoubtedly one of those significant steps towards a better, sustainable future.

Easy DIY Composting Guide

Selecting your compost location

Transforming your kitchen into a zero-waste haven starts with employing a profound understanding and effective management of waste. It's about acknowledging that waste production is an undesired by-product of our usual cooking and eating practices, and considering how we can diminish or completely neutralize its impact.

The first step in the waste management hierarchy is always the reduction of waste – reducing the volume of waste that your kitchen produces. It can be facilitated by a wide array of strategies like mindful shopping, smart storage, and creative use of leftovers. However, even with the most thorough waste reduction plans, it's most likely that at the end of the day, there will be some form of waste generated.

That's where composting comes into play. Composting is a natural process where organic waste materials decompose to create nutrient-rich soil that can be used for planting various kinds of vegetation. It's nature's own recycling scheme, turning kitchen scraps - which could have easily ended up in landfill - into a profitable resource for creating lush, vigorous plant growth.

Before you begin with composting, one essential step is to select the appropriate location for your composting bin or pile. It can be either outdoors or indoors, depending on your situation and preference. An outdoor compost pile enjoys the benefits of aeration from wind and decomposition assistance from native microorganisms, insects, and worms. Meanwhile, an indoor compost bin, under the kitchen sink or in the garage for example, can be a practical choice for those who have limited outdoor space or live in an urban setting.

If you choose an outdoor location, make sure it's a place that gets a mix of sun and shade, and is easily accessible year-round. Also, consider a location near a water source to maintain the compost pile's moisture.

For indoor composting, select a location that is convenient and easily accessible but out of the way of daily activities. Also, remember to choose a container with a tight-fitting lid to prevent any smells or flies and consider a model with a filter for added odor control if you are concerned about possible smells.

Setting up a composting system in your zero-waste kitchen requires some thought and preparation, but once it becomes a regular part of your kitchen routine, it will feel simple and seamless. Not only does it reduce your kitchen's waste drastically, but it also provides you with rich, healthy soil for your plants.

The journey towards a zero-waste kitchen may take time, but every small change you introduce brings us all a step closer to a sustainable future. With holistic waste management strategies and practical DIY composting, your eco-friendly haven is within reach.

Choosing the right compost materials

A zero-waste kitchen is more than a mere concept; it is a lifestyle decision that reflects your commitment to the environment, sustainability, and the world. Taking the initial steps towards this lifestyle change can often feel overwhelming, especially when it comes to dealing with waste. However, time and careful intervention can convert the most cluttered kitchen into a model of efficiency and ecological friendliness.

One of the most effective methods of dealing with kitchen waste is composting. Composting is an easy and cost-effective method to manage waste while generating nutrient-rich material for your plants. Moreover, composting effectively diverts as much as 30% of household waste away from the garbage bin and towards something vastly more beneficial.

Creating compost at home is a straightforward process requiring minimal space, making it the perfect solution for urban dwellers. A simple container with a lid, stored either indoors or outdoors, would usually suffice. Done correctly, composting is also a clean and odorless procedure, a far cry from the assumptions of many skeptics.

What can you compost? The list might surprise you.

Kitchen waste is at the top of the compostable list, because it includes many things you would normally throw away: vegetable peels, coffee grounds, loose tea leaves, stale bread, and eggshells. You can also compost small amounts of newspaper, wooden toothpicks, and, surprisingly, hair and fur. Garden waste, such as grass trimmings or fallen leaves, also makes excellent compost material.

However, not all kitchen waste is compostable. Avoid adding meats or dairy products to your compost bins as they emit unsavory odors and can attract pests. Processed foods, sauces, oils, and diseased plants should also be left out of your compost pile.

Overall, composting is not just a means of waste disposal. It's an approach of converting waste into valuable resources, which supports the concept of the zero-waste kitchen. By implementing these practices, your kitchen can become an eco-friendly haven, contributing significantly to the health of our planet.

Choosing and sticking with a sustainable lifestyle might need rigorous commitment, but the rewards of maintaining a zero-waste kitchen are immense - for you and the Earth. As you continue on this journey, remember, each step you take towards reducing waste is a step towards a healthier, more sustainable world.

Setting up an indoor composting

Promoting a zero-waste lifestyle is the need of the hour. As climate change and scarcity of resources become pressing issues, it is incumbent upon each one of us to do our part in making our planet a more sustainable place for future generations to inhabit. Your commitment to a zero-waste kitchen is a significant step toward this goal. Starting with your kitchen waste is a smart choice because it's often the biggest source of waste in a typical household. One of the easiest methods of using this waste is composting. This process can seem daunting to most people who are unfamiliar with the process. However, with a few easy and manageable steps, any novice can become successful at making and managing DIY compost.

Step 1: Choose Your Composter

There is an array of composters available on the market. Choose one that suits your needs and space in your kitchen. Compost bins come in different sizes, designs, and materials. Some are aesthetic enough to sit on your kitchen counter, while others are designed to be practical and efficient.

Step 2: Understand the Components

Composting is no less than a science experiment happening right in your bin. Largely, composting is the process of turning organic materials, mostly your kitchen scraps, into nutrient-rich soil. For the process to happen properly, you will need green ingredients - which include your vegetable and fruit peels, coffee grounds, tea bags, fresh grass clippings, and brown ingredients – which primarily involve dry leaves, twigs, paper, cardboard, etc. You will need to mix these for the composting process to take place.

Step 3: Assemble Your Compost Bin

Begin layering your compost bin - first with browns then with greens. Always try to maintain a balance, although it doesn't need to be perfect. As you toss in your kitchen scraps, cover them with a layer of browns. Mix it occasionally for aeration.

Step 4: Care for Your Compost

While the composting process is mostly self-driven, it does require some basic care. Ensure the compost is moist but not wet. Too much water can smother the pile. Turn the compost often to allow air into the system, which helps in breaking down the material.

Step 5: Harvest Your Compost

Once your compost bin is full and the waste has decomposed, it's time to harvest. Screening your compost can separate the finished product from any unprocessed materials. The result is a rich, crumbly compost that is ready to be repurposed.

Turning your kitchen into a zero-waste zone is a journey and not a destination. Along the way, you will learn new skills like composting and find the joy in minimizing your ecological impact. Whether you are an experienced eco-warrior or a recent convert, transforming your cooking space into an eco-friendly haven is a venture worth pursuing.

Maintaining your compost pile

In the pursuit of a zero-waste kitchen, one cannot overlook the eventual generation of waste. Even with careful planning and conscious purchasing, organic waste from cooking is inevitable. However, this waste doesn't have to end up in landfills. It can serve a significantly beneficial purpose: composting. Composting is a crucial feature of a zero-waste kitchen, transforming your everyday organic waste into nutrient-rich soil for your garden. In itself, composting is a remarkable action towards sustainability and waste prevention, contributing enormously to achieving a zero-waste kitchen.

So how does one begin composting at home? While it might seem daunting initially, it is, in fact, a straightforward process that anyone can uphold in their cooking space. The first step typically involves a compost bin, which can be an upcycled container lying around your house, or something bought specifically for the purpose. It need not be large, especially if you are just starting; find something that fits comfortably in your kitchen's available space. The bin must have a lid to control odors and should be lined with compostable liners for easy removal of compost.

Composting requires a balance of green and brown materials. Green materials are full of nitrogen and include items such as vegetable peels, coffee grounds, or grass clippings; they help to speed up the composting process. Conversely, brown materials, such as dead leaves, wood chips, and cardboard or paper products, provide carbon and assist in balancing out the composition. A suitable ratio to try achieving is two-thirds brown materials to one-third green materials.

To maintain your compost pile, you would need to turn or mix the materials in your bin weekly to enhance aeration. This helps to accelerate decomposition by allowing bacteria to break down the organic matter more efficiently. In a balanced compost heap, no foul odor should emanate; if it does, it might indicate too many green materials and requires more brown materials to restore balance.

Compost is ready when it turns into a dark, earthy substance that resembles garden soil. This process can take anywhere between two weeks to two months, depending on the materials used and the conducive environment maintained. Once ready, you can add this compost to your garden soil and reap the benefits of a nutritious mix, fostering healthy plant growth.

Thus, a zero-waste kitchen can contribute to the creation of an eco-friendly haven right in your backyard. Composting serves a dual purpose of waste reduction and enhancement of soil fertility. With a little patience and responsibility, you can do your part in curbing the global waste problem and sustaining the earth, one kitchen at a time.

Utilizing compost in the kitchen

Are you tired of looking at overflowing trash bins and realizing the immensity of the waste generated in your kitchen? Transformative kitchen practices can be an antidote to our waste crisis, placing us on the more sustainable limelight of a zero-waste kitchen - one of the most prominent being composting. This chapter delves into the ins and outs of dealing with waste in a zero-waste kitchen, with a spotlight on an easy DIY composting guide and utilizing compost in the kitchen.

First and foremost, understanding the type of waste generated in your kitchen is key. Broadly, kitchen waste can be categorized into food waste (fruits, vegetables, coffee grounds) and non-food waste (plastic, paper). A zero-waste kitchen aims to drastically reduce, if not eliminate, the production of such waste, especially non-food waste. Composting happens to be the most common method used in handling food waste.

Composting, in its most basic form, is a natural process that turns your kitchen waste into a rich soil conditioner. It's a simple action that can have a profound impact on waste reduction. DIY composting starts with designating a dedicated compost bin or pile in your backyard or, if you're up for the challenge, inside your kitchen. There are numerous compact composting bins available in the market that can fit under your kitchen sink.

To start composting, mix green waste - which includes fruit and vegetable scraps, coffee grounds, tea bags - and brown waste - which include fallen leaves, paper, cardboard. The key is to maintain a healthy balance between these green and brown waste, usually a ratio of 1:2. Ensure your compost heap is turned over regularly for the purpose of aeration, which accelerates the composting process.

Once your compost is ready, which can take anywhere between 2 weeks to 2 months, depending upon your composting method, it's time to utilize it in your kitchen. The term "black gold" has often been used to refer to compost due to its immense value in enriching soil and boosting plant growth.

If you have indoor plants, use this nutrient-rich compost to feed them. Should your kitchen be blessed with a small herb or vegetable garden, apply it as a soil conditioner. Compost not only provides essential nutrients to your plants, but also improves the soil structure, supporting better water retention and healthier root development.

In conclusion, composting is more than just a way of curbing kitchen waste; it's about forging a closer relationship with the very nature that sustains us. It is about viewing waste not as something to dispose of, but as a stockpile of resources that, if used wisely, can impart significant health and environmental benefits. Adopting the practice of composting in a zero-waste kitchen can create a substantial difference in our waste management strategies, recalibrating our relationship with food and its aftermath to hand us a more sustainable, viable future.

In the chapters to follow, we will explore more such practices to guide you in your journey towards a Zero-waste Kitchen – a comprehensive movement towards an eco-friendly haven.

Alternative Solutions for Waste

Composting Organic Kitchen Waste

Taking the path toward a zero-waste kitchen requires a singular focus on how we manage waste. Traditionally, our approach to handling waste is characterized by a linear model—wherein we 'take, make, and dispose'. However, zero-waste necessitates a systemic shift to a circular model that emphasizes 'reduce, reuse, and recycle'.

Dealing with waste in a zero-waste kitchen involves a significant transition from the typical kitchen setup. The aim is the complete elimination of waste—not simply moved out of sight into the bin, but genuinely abolished. How then, do we deal with inevitable waste created in our cooking spaces?

The answer lies in viewing waste as a resource rather than a burden. Waste produced in the kitchen is largely organic and has the potential to be recycled back into the environment. The process of composting serves as an excellent solution to this problem.

Composting is the biological decomposition of organic wastes under controlled conditions to produce a humus-like, nutrient-rich material. It offers a sustainable alternative to disposing of food waste in landfills. Kitchen wastes such as fruit and vegetable peels, coffee grounds, eggshells, tea bags, and even paper napkins serve as ideal materials for composting.

Composting not only helps reduce landfill waste, but it can also significantly cut down greenhouse gas emissions by preventing the release of harmful methane gas. Furthermore, the compost material produced is a rich, fertile substance that can be used to enhance the growth of plants and crops. Thus, incorporating composting into your kitchen not only aids in maintaining a zero-waste setup but also contributes positively to the environment.

Apart from composting, there are other ways to deal with kitchen waste. For instance, certain wastes like coffee grounds and eggshells can be directly used as soil fertilizer. Not to mention, cooking oil can be collected and sent to facilities to be converted into biofuel.

Indeed, the journey toward a zero-waste kitchen is an ongoing process and might seem daunting at first glance. However, remember that each small step, each minor change, contributes to a broader, global impact. It is simply about restructuring our habits to align with responsible waste management practices.

That is our solemn responsibility to our planet—a responsibility that begins at the core of our homes, our kitchens.

Upcycling Food Containers

In the realm of the culinary arts, the kitchen is often revered as the heart of the home–a versatile, bustling hub that nourishes body and soul. However, for all its merits, the kitchen is invariably a primary source of household waste. Given the urgent conversations surrounding environmental preservation, the concept of the 'Zero-waste Kitchen' has emerged as a compelling response, inviting the aspiring eco-enthusiast to minimize waste produced in their culinary habitat.

A Zero-waste Kitchen is not built overnight–it is a shift in mindset, a gradual engagement with eco-friendliness that redefines the relationship between cooking space and waste, grounded in three principles: reduction, reuse, and recycle. Admittedly, complete elimination of waste might not be feasible, but it is certainly possible to aim for a low waste kitchen.

To truly embrace a Zero-waste Kitchen, it's important to first understand the nature of kitchen waste. Understanding of what kitchen waste constitutes is our first step towards minimizing it. Predominantly, kitchen waste is either packaging waste from groceries and ingredients, or food waste from leftover meals and food scraps. Armed with this understanding, you can look at converting this waste into value instead of letting it mindlessly accumulate in landfills.

Opt for bulk buying, bringing your own containers, bags and shopping from local markets which avoid unnecessary packaging. Reuse any unavoidable packaging that comes your way. For instance, a glass pasta sauce jar could find a second life as a cereal dispenser, a terrarium, or even a quaint flower vase. By choosing to reinvent the usage scenario for these items, you not only reduce waste but also discover multifunctional uses for everyday items.

When it comes to food waste, there are a multitude of creative solutions. One certainly is composting, converting organic matter like vegetable peels, coffee grounds, and eggshells into nutrient-rich soil amendment good for your plants. For unavoidable waste like bones or shells, consider making broths or infusions.

Upcycling food containers is yet another strategy to reduce waste in the kitchen. Upcycling, which extends an object's life by repurposing it for a different use, is a unique blend of creativity, utility, and eco-friendliness. Old utensil canisters, for example, could become planting pots, pencil holders, or even artistic candle holders. Potential upcycling projects depend solely upon the imagination, transforming what was once a 'waste' into something practical, beautiful, and most importantly, sustainable.

In essence, transforming your cooking space into an Eco-friendly haven doesn't merely revolve around the switch to organic products or energy-saving appliances– it is a multifaceted journey involving meticulous waste management, creative upcycling, and a continuous dedication towards sustainability. Adopting a Zero-waste Kitchen is, after all, an affirmation of our shared responsibility towards preserving the planet for future generations.

Donating Unused Ingredients

Creating a zero-waste kitchen requires innovative action to deal with the inevitable byproducts of our culinary endeavors. Rather than allowing waste to end up in a landfill, we should explore alternative solutions to create a sustainable and eco-friendly cooking haven. Wasted food represents not just squandered nutritional potential, but also a needless drain on our planet's valuable resources. It is time to develop a new mindset.

Firstly, it is important to understand that, in a zero-waste kitchen, our aim is not to cease producing any waste at all. This would be an impossible goal, especially considering that even the act of cooking produces unavoidable waste such as peels, cores, and seeds. Instead, our goal is to minimize unnecessary waste and find constructive uses for our unavoidable waste.

To repurpose unavoidable waste, composting is a great solution. Contrary to popular assumption, composting does not necessarily require a garden or a large amount of space. Even those in urban apartments can compost by using an indoor compost bin, which contains the waste and its odors. A compost bin turns kitchen scraps into nutrient-rich soil that can be used to grow herbs, vegetables, and other plants.

If composting is not an option, the kitchen scraps can also be put to other uses. For example, vegetable and fruit peels can be used to make homemade broths, while eggshells can be ground down and used to provide calcium to plants. There is a wealth of creative ways to put our kitchen waste to good use.

Unused ingredients, on the other hand, can often find a better destination. How many times have we bought too much of a particular ingredient, only to have it spoil and be thrown away? One simple solution is planning our meals and grocery shopping carefully, so we buy only what we need.

However, there will inevitably be times when we end up with too much. In such instances, consider donating these ingredients. Many food banks and charities gratefully accept unopened, non-perishable foods. Some charities even have the facilities to accept perishable food as long as it hasn't expired, so it's worth inquiring about this possibility.

It's also worth embracing preservation methods, such as canning, pickling, freezing, and dehydrating, to extend the life of surplus foods. This way, you'll always have a ready supply of ingredients without worrying about them spoiling.

Remember, every small step we take toward a zero-waste kitchen has a major impact. We can all play a part in creating a more sustainable future. By considering alternative solutions for kitchen waste, we change our patterns of consumption, decrease our negative impact on the environment, and contribute to a healthier planet.

Drying Out Leftovers

The kitchen is the heartbeat of every home. It's where meals are made, discussions are held, and memories are crafted with love. Amidst these activities, the kitchen inevitably becomes the epicenter of one undesirable by-product - waste. The Zero-waste Kitchen seeks to guide you in transforming your kitchen's potential wasteland into a niche eco-friendly haven.

So, how do we deal with waste in a Zero-waste Kitchen? The answer lies in adopting comprehensive and alternative solutions that can seamlessly merge with your daily culinary rituals. Simply put, the mission is not waste elimination but waste management.

Indeed, the journey towards a Zero-waste Kitchen doesn't necessarily mean a complete upending of your customary practices but rather a series of small, intelligent tweaks.

Take, for example, your kitchen leftovers. Often, we are quick to label our uneaten foods as waste, tossing them into the trash bin without a second thought. But here, perspective is paramount. In the Zero-waste Kitchen, leftovers are not seen as waste but rather as potential avenues for delicious new meals or, interestingly enough, dried out treats.

The process of drying out leftovers is efficient and straightforward, essentially extending the life of your food and reducing the amount of food bin bound. Whether it's fruits, vegetables, herbs or even certain meats, a low-heat oven or a food dehydrator can work wonders. Once properly dried, these foods can be stored for months, ready to be used in varying future dishes or snacks. This proves a double-win, as it preserves the precious resources embedded in our food while offering a cost-effective solution for mindful homeowners.

Going even further, certain leftovers that can't be dried and repurposed for human consumption, such as vegetable scraps or fruit peels, are not necessarily waste just yet. As it turns out, these scraps make excellent nutrient-rich food for worms in a worm farm or as composting material for your home garden, or even your indoor plants. To be precise, the 'waste' in your kitchen becomes beneficial additions elsewhere in your home, allowing you to complete the circle of a sustainable lifestyle.

Undeniably, the path towards a Zero-waste Kitchen is a voyage of unlearning, relearning, and making a conscious choice every step of the way. It is the manifestation of the belief that eco-friendly practices start from the confines of our own homes. The aim then becomes not to leave zero-waste, but around our daily routines, to weave a veil of mindfulness that takes into account the impact our choices bear on our planet.

This, then, is the essence of 'The Zero-waste Kitchen': not an end, but a continuous journey towards the environmental consciousness that transforms small individual efforts into the mighty collective endeavor to protect and preserve our only home, the Earth.

Implementing Worm Farming

The zero-waste kitchen, as the name implies, unabashedly embraces the concept of leaving no resource unutilized, with the intent of minimizing waste and nurturing environmental sustainability. Indeed, a zero-waste kitchen may initially seem to be an audacious proposition; however, with concerted effort, careful planning, and strategic management, it is certainly attainable. This chapter aims to broaden your understanding and spark creativity as we discuss various alternative solutions for waste as well as explore the remarkable technique of worm farming.

Intuitively, the first step to achieving a zero-waste kitchen revolves around the concept of smart shopping. The judicious selection of products that have the least packaging, buying in bulk whenever feasible, prioritizing organic produce, and using your own reusable bags and containers can significantly downsize the volume of waste generated. Coupled with this, habits such as composting kitchen waste, separating and recycling, and reusing items whenever possible tilt the odds favorably towards a zero-waste kitchen.

Let us now delve into some of the alternative solutions for food leftovers and waste. Rather than discarding scraps and peels, consider creatively incorporating them back into your meals or composting them to create natural fertilizers. Coffee grounds and eggshells, for instance, serve as excellent additions to enrich the compost pile, and vegetable scraps can be used to make nutrient-rich broths.

A further step to redefine waste in your kitchen involves harnessing the power of waste by converting it into energy. This can be achieved through the method of Anaerobic Digestion (AD), where organic waste materials are broken down to produce biogas - a renewable energy source. Although this may seem daunting, small-scale, home-friendly AD systems are making this process more accessible.

Finally, one approach that warrants particular attention is worm farming, otherwise known as vermiculture. Vermiculture facilitates the conversion of organic kitchen waste into worm castings - a rich, fertile compost that is excellent for plants. Setting up your own worm farm might seem like an intricate process, but it is surprisingly straightforward. All you need is a dark container, moisture-absorbing bedding like shredded newspaper, vegetable scraps, a batch of composting worms, and a little patience. As these worms consume organic materials, they expel castings that are highly beneficial to soil health. The worms reproduce on the farm, thus providing a sustainable solution for organic waste management.

In conclusion, a zero-waste kitchen hinges on a drastic mindset shift along with daily committed action. It is a transformative journey that requires careful consideration and determined practice. However, with the immensely positive impact it creates on the environment and our health, the rewards far outweigh the initial efforts. This process also reinforces the importance of sustainable living while illustrating that every individual effort counts towards a greener, healthier planet.

BECOMING ADVOCATES FOR ZERO-WASTE LIVING

Sharing your Journey

Highlight Personal Successes

This book is about embracing and embodying a shift in mindset, not just about imparting a set of instructions for more sustainable living. One of the most powerful tools in inspiring change is through sharing personal stories, experiences, and successes.

We are not just concerned with decreasing our individual carbon footprints, we have chosen to take on a more substantial role, becoming advocates for zero-waste living. We are agents who foster and incite change in our communities and in the everyday lives of people we encounter.

Sharing your journey not only shapes how people perceive sustainable lifestyles, but also allows them to witness firsthand how living an eco-friendly life is both manageable and rewarding. Oftentimes, the concept of zero-waste living can seem daunting and impractical, gathering misconceptions and doubts from those unfamiliar with the movement. Let's dispel these misconceptions and replace them with a profound appreciation of the incredible capacity of individual action to inspire global change.

When we share our journeys, we open ourselves up to a bevy of learning and growth opportunities. There's always room for new ideas and improvements and involvement in the zero-waste community can offer a valuable pool of knowledge from which to draw.

Remember, every step you take towards reducing waste is a success. Don't be shy about highlighting these personal achievements, no matter how small. Did you transition from a traditional plastic dish scrub to one made of sustainable materials? That's a win. Did you convince a friend to try out a zero-waste grocery shopping technique? That's another win.

Every step forward, no matter how small, brings us closer to the goal of a more sustainable, zero-waste world. Sharing your successes has a two-fold effect; it rewards you with much-deserved recognition and motivates others to adopt similar practices.

By sharing your journey and highlighting your personal successes, you contribute to an ever-expanding movement that is redefining how we interact with the world around us. You become an integral part of a community dedicated to minimizing damage to our environment and ensure a healthier future for generations to come. It may not always be easy, but the rewards of manifesting your commitment into tangible change are both significant and incredibly inspiring.

Discuss Challenges Overcome

Embracing the zero-waste lifestyle signals a substantial shift in the manner one perceives and interacts with their environment. Resorting to a low-impact way of life requires conscientiousness, commitment, and conscious behavior alterations towards sustainability and conservation. It's far beyond decluttering and minimalism - it's about generating minimal waste that may eventually burden our planet. And once you make this transition, one cannot and indeed should not limit this wisdom to oneself. This book, therefore, emphasizes the importance of becoming advocates for zero-waste living and sharing your journey with others.

Leading a zero-waste lifestyle is, in essence, a personal journey. Along the way, you discover newer ways to recycle, upcycle, and sustain by not contributing waste. Sharing these experiences and spreading the word can inspire others and make a significant difference. In today's digital world, it's not hard to find platforms to share your journey. Social media and blogging platforms connect you with people worldwide, allowing you to share your experiences, hacks, insights, and even challenges encountered during your zero-waste endeavor. The objective here is not just to flaunt your effort, but to inspire, empower, and motivate others to adopt this lifestyle.

One common misconception about zero-waste living is a seamless and effortless shift. No substantial change comes without its hurdles and challenges, and this lifestyle transformation is not immune to them. Initially, you may struggle with getting rid of habits that contribute to waste generation. The desire for quick, easy, and conveniently packaged food can be challenging. Moreover, zero-waste choices may not always be cost-effective and can present financial constraints especially when accommodating organic and locally sourced produce.

Practical challenges also involve finding suitable replacements for daily use items that are environmentally friendly, biodegradable, and within your budget. While manufacturers are producing earth-friendly alternatives, they may not always be readily available or affordable. Hence, it requires profound planning and resourcefulness to fully equip your kitchen with viable, sustainable options.

However, it's important to remember that every journey is unique and subjective. Overcoming these challenges does not warrant perfection, but perseverance. It's not about achieving entirely zero-waste living but reducing the waste generated to a bare minimum. Sharing these challenges, how they were or weren't overcome, doesn't illustrate failure, but encourages resilience among others embarking on their journey.

Such advocacy works like a chain reaction. You share your experiences and ignite interests, those listening share it forward, which multiplies the impact manifolds. Remember, adopting a zero-waste lifestyle may start as a personal choice, but it has the potential to sow seeds for a global impact. Therefore, as you undertake this journey, take it upon yourself to educate, motivate, and inspire others to join the movement. Not only will you be reducing your footprint, but you may also influence others to reduce theirs too, gradually inching towards a cleaner, greener planet.

Explain Zero-waste Benefits

In the transformative journey to a zero-waste kitchen, one of the most invaluable roles you will fulfill is that of an advocate for sustainable living. As you adopt eco-friendly practices and change your cooking space into an environmentally friendly haven, you can use your experience and knowledge to spark a domino effect. Light the path for friends, family, colleagues, and the local community to also embrace the principles of zero-waste -- essentially becoming an advocate for this life-altering movement.

Sharing your journey epitomizes the saying 'actions speak louder than words.' By illustrating the practicalities, challenges, and accomplishments of the zero-waste lifestyle, you become a living testimony that a sustainable kitchen is viable and beneficial. Regularly share your experiences via social media, community groups, or simple conversations. This can inspire others to join the movement and amplify the impact on our environment.

This brings us to the vital point of communicating the benefits of zero-waste living. More than just an eco-friendly movement, zero-waste living offers substantial benefits on multiple fronts.

Firstly, it helps to minimize the impact of kitchen activities on the environment, by reducing waste generation and limiting the reliance on non-renewable resources. In a world fighting to curb pollution, and to slow down climate change, zero-waste kitchens become part of the solution, rather than contributing to the problem.

Secondly, zero-waste living presents opportunities for financial savings. Many standard commercial kitchen products are replaced with sustainable, reusable alternatives, reducing overall expenditures in the long run. It also encourages mindful consumerism, a practice where purchases are thoughtfully considered before being made, a habit that redirects funds from being spent on unnecessary items.

Moreover, a zero-waste lifestyle sparks inventiveness and encourages healthier eating habits. By avoiding processed and packaged foods, your diet often shifts towards whole and fresh ingredients. This inadvertently boosts your health, well-being, and overall quality of life.

When taking the mantle of being an advocate for zero-waste living, focus your energy on highlighting these benefits and your personal journey in propagating this message. Your foundation in actual practice will provide credibility and inspire others to adopt this lifestyle, thereby not only making a difference in your life but also in the lives of others and the planet at large.

Provide Practical Advice

Becoming an advocate for zero-waste living is a transformative journey that weaves together practical skills and a deep commitment to preserving the environment. As we venture into this exciting way of life, we embark on a path less travelled —one that may be strewn with trials and triumphs—but ultimately a way of life that plays a pivotal role in reducing the escalating burden on our planet.

Sharing this journey, particularly the lessons we learn along the way, serves as an influencing tool that can be used to encourage others to adopt a similar approach. And what better place to start sharing this journey than by transforming our kitchens into eco-friendly sanctuaries?

Modern kitchens are often shrines to convenience, replete with disposable products and over-packaged items that contribute to alarming levels of waste. The wasteful practices hindering most kitchens are largely influenced by the consumer-driven world we've grown accustomed to and the desire for fast and easy solutions. However, by electing to turn your kitchen into a zero-waste haven, not only do you directly combat against excessive waste production, but you also demonstrate to others that an eco-friendly lifestyle is both attainable and rewarding.

Starting your zero-waste journey requires patience, determination, and a radical rethink of your consumption practices. Begin by conducting a waste audit to understand the magnitude of waste generated in your kitchen, ranging from food leftovers to plastic packaging. Assess this waste critically, questioning whether these items were necessary and how they can be substituted for reusable or compostable options.

Upon identifying the major sources of waste, procure eco-friendly alternatives. Opt for glass containers and jars instead of single-use plastic bags. Consider investing in a compost bin instead of discarding your food waste. Keep a tab on your shopping habits and aim for loose, package-free produce whenever possible. Remember, small changes accumulated over time make a huge impact.

While on this zero-waste journey, it's crucial to share your experiences, both successes and failures, with the community around you. Emphasize the importance of taking collective action and the role each individual can play in bringing about a societal shift towards a zero-waste mindset. Bolstered by your practical experience, provide clear, concise, and actionable advice, making lifestyle changes feel less daunting and more achievable for those around you.

Becoming an advocate for zero-waste living means more than just reducing waste — it means fostering a sustainable lifestyle, inspiring change, and contributing to a greener, healthier planet. Take every opportunity to lead by example, share your journey, and provide practical advice - thereby investing as much in the people around you as you are in the environment.

Encourage Community Involvement

Embracing a zero-waste lifestyle begins from within. However, it doesn't have to end there. Zero-waste living can proliferate across communities, cities, and countries when those who have embraced this lifestyle become advocates. This chapter will explore how you, as a champion of zero-waste living, can share your journey to encourage community involvement.

As an ardent practitioner of zero-waste living, sharing your journey can be incredibly powerful. It presents a tangible example of the positive changes and simultaneous challenges a zero-waste lifestyle can entail. Sharing your journey isn't about boasting achievements; it's about communicating what you've learnt during your journey, showing the benefits and challenges, offering a realistic view of how it's possible to function sustainably in a world not yet designed for zero-waste.

There are myriad ways to share your journey. It can be as simple as having a conversation with friends or writing a blog post to reach out to people beyond your immediate circle. Social media platforms can serve as influential channels to share tips, insights, and personal experiences about reducing waste in the kitchen. Remember, the intent is to inspire and engage others, not push them to instantly eliminate all their waste.

Part of sharing is also being open to learning from others. A community of like-minded people can offer incredible support, insights and ideas. Hosting or partaking in forums, workshops, or group discussions can lead to sharing of unique experiences, expanding your perspective whilst at the same time, strengthening the community's resolve to adopt the zero-waste lifestyle.

Encouraging community involvement goes a step beyond

sharing. Think about how you can bring the sustainable practices you've adopted in your kitchen to a wider group of people. Organize community swap events to exchange unused kitchen items, introduce a collection system for compostable kitchen waste, encourage local businesses to use eco-friendly packaging, or start a community garden. Your actions, big or small, can positively impact your community's environmental footprint and may influence others to follow your lead.

Remember, the journey to a zero-waste kitchen and eventually a zero-waste lifestyle is a continuous process of learning and growth. It's a path threaded with realizations around the true cost of convenience and throw-away culture. Therefore, as an advocate, your role will be to inspire, motivate, and lead by example. When you involve the community, it becomes less about personal gain and more about collective environmental prosperity.

In conclusion, becoming an advocate for zero-waste living involves sharing your journey and providing guidance to those willing to transform their kitchens – and their lives – into places of sustainability. It's about truly believing in the potential of individuals to make significant lifestyle changes and the potential of communities to foster an overall environment of change. This is how we can make the idea of a zero-waste kitchen, and eventually, a zero-waste world, a reality.

Engaging with the Community

Promote local sustainable businesses

In the course of our lives, we hold innumerable roles. From parents to professionals, our daily endeavors are marked by our identification with these roles. Adding yet another to this list should not be daunting but encouraging advocates for zero-waste living. This is an identity that does not compete with our extant roles, rather it complements them, cutting across domains, and putting a unique perspective on our interactions.

As we begin to adopt a zero-waste lifestyle in our kitchens, it is but natural for this ethos to percolate into other facets of our lives. We start to examine our everyday actions and decisions in light of their environmental impact. The proximity of this identification to our everyday lives makes us potent advocates, with the ability to show our communities the benefits of sustainable living, both immediate and far-reaching.

Embracing and promulgating zero-waste living also ushers us into a new community of eco-conscious people. This community is marked by both a shared commitment to sustainable living and a unique diversity, where people from different walks of life come together with their unique perspectives and insights. Contributing to this community not only enriches us personally, but also fortifies the collective effort towards sustainable living.

One of the ways in which we can contribute meaningfully to this community is by promoting local sustainable businesses. By frequenting these businesses, we are strengthening the local economy, reducing carbon footprint associated with long-distance transportation, and encouraging practices that are in line with our eco-friendly lifestyle. These businesses often offer inspiring stories of sustainable initiatives, and by choosing to patronize them, we are essentially casting a vote for the kind of world we wish to inhabit.

As the popular maxim goes - we vote with our wallets. Every purchase we make sends a potent message about the sort of practices we support. By choosing local, organic, and fair-trade options, we are actively supporting a sustainable model of production and consumption. Moreover, engaging with these businesses gives us the opportunity to educate others about the importance and feasibility of sustainable living.

Becoming advocates for zero-waste living might appear challenging initially. However, as we engage with our communities, share our stories, and listen to the journeys of others, we realize the boundless possibilities that come with this title - the ability to catalyze change, to inspire others, and most importantly, to contribute meaningfully towards building a sustainable future for the world. It is, without a doubt, a role worth embracing.

Organize zero-waste workshops

Zero-waste Living is not just a fad or a trend. It is an ethos. It demands the commitment to reduce what we take, recycle and throw away. As an individual, you are responsible for making conscious efforts to alleviate the overburdened planet.

Vital to the transition towards a Zero-waste Kitchen is an understanding of how our habits impact the environment. Pioneering a shift from mindless consumption to thoughtful sustainability, the Zero-waste Kitchen is as much about making smart choices as it is about ecological responsibility.

Fostering such a transformation also requires us to go beyond the personal sphere and engage with our community. Efforts for a sustainable kitchen and home are most effective when they are part of a larger circle of influence.

One such way to engage your community is by organizing Zero-waste Workshops. Not only do these workshops serve as a platform to spread awareness about sustainable living, but they also provide actionable tips and procedures for minimizing waste.

Workshops can include hands-on, practical sessions on home composting, green shopping habits, DIY eco-friendly kitchen cleaners, among others. They may also include panel discussions featuring local Zero-waste advocates, organic farmers, and sustainability experts. Moreover, these workshops could be an opportunity to invite local businesses that offer eco-friendly products and services, facilitating the transition towards sustainable living within the community.

Such collective efforts would instill an ethos of conscious consumption and waste management, and in turn, have a more profound impact. Remember, the goal is not for one person to do Zero-waste perfectly but for millions of people to do it imperfectly.

Success, in this endeavor, lies not in rigid adherence to the ethos but in the widespread, incremental adoption of sustainable practices. Pledge for a Zero-waste Kitchen, share your journey, and inspire those around you. As you light the path for others, you inadvertently tread further along your path towards sustainable living.

Embrace the journey of transforming your kitchen into an eco-friendly haven and let it inspire others to follow suit. The Zero-waste Kitchen is not just about waste reduction, it's a conversation starter, an advocacy tool, and a strong testament to your commitment to preserving our planet.

Involve in policy change

Our journey toward operating zero-waste kitchens isn't restricted to the four walls of our own homes but extends to the society we inhabit. It involves becoming advocates for a broader culture of low waste living and engaging with the community at a grassroots level.

Adopting the zero-waste lifestyle means transforming our mindset toward resources, viewing them as invaluable and non-expandable. This conviction keeps us from perceiving anything as dispensable, and therefore waste. To share this innovative philosophy with others and promote its principles in our community is the first step toward becoming a zero-waste advocate.

We can begin by spreading awareness about the zero-waste lifestyle and the impact it has on our environment, health, and future. This can be achieved through town meetings, local groups, social media platforms, or community newsletters.

It's important to emphasize that every small change matters. Often, people are hesitant about embracing waste-free living because it seems daunting, if not impossible. However, it's crucial to communicate that even the smallest changes contribute significantly towards the end goal. Initiating a conversation about a reusable shopping bag's potential benefits or demonstrating how to compost leftover food at home could open avenues for deeper discussions and broader societal changes.

Implementing the Zero-waste principle goes beyond individual habits and demands systematic changes. As advocates, we can start by pressing our local representatives for smarter, eco-friendly policies. Municipalities could be encouraged to develop composting facilities or provide support for farmers' markets which largely eliminate the need for packaged goods.

We need to actively get involved in policy change. This might mean attending town hall meetings, writing to your local government representative, advocating for regulations that discourage single-use plastics, or getting involved with non-profit organizations that focus on waste reduction.

It's not just about transforming our own kitchens but fostering an entire community of zero waste. Encouraging restaurants, grocery stores, and schools to adopt sustainable practices and reduce their waste would also further positive change.

It takes courage, commitment, and resilience to step up as advocates for zero-waste living. We might face resistance, skepticism, and challenges along the way. But remember, every great movement began with a single step. As individuals, families, and communities, we have the power to drive that change toward a sustainable, waste-free future.

Together, let's redefine our relationship with waste and transform our kitchens, our communities, and ultimately, our world into eco-friendly havens.

Initiate neighborhood clean-ups

Embracing a zero-waste lifestyle extends far beyond individual habits; it is about fostering a collective change within communities. Whether you're just starting your zero-waste journey or have been an avid advocate for many years, there is much you can do to inspire others to help create a more sustainable world, beginning right within your kitchen.

First, consider taking actions that allow fellow community members to witness the possibilities and benefits of zero-waste living firsthand. You might, for instance, launch a local initiative focused on reducing food waste. This could involve organizing workshops that educate participants on better food storage techniques, intelligent grocery shopping, creating meal plans that minimize waste, composting, and creatively using food scraps.

Becoming a zero-waste advocate also involves engaging with local businesses and government regulations. Understand that fostering corporate responsibility towards zero-waste is just as important as individual change. Encourage local restaurants and grocery stores to rethink their waste policies. This may entail promoting ideas like offering discounts for customers who bring their own containers or lobbying for local regulations that limit single-use plastics.

Diving deeper, initiate neighborhood clean-ups. These get-togethers not only contribute towards maintaining cleaner surroundings but also serve as educational experiences. They expose community members to the sheer volume of waste produced and dumped, which not only affects us but also negatively impacts wildlife, and the overall health of our planet.

By incorporating activities like these, zero-waste living will become a genuine community effort. The process of bringing about change is slow, but every single step counts. Acting as advocates for the zero-waste movement, we can guide those around us to make better choices and inspire them to play their part in protecting our planet for future generations.

Undoubtedly, the zero-waste journey in your kitchen begins with you, but its influence has the potential to infiltrate your neighborhood and beyond, ultimately driving a change in the world at large. Because a zero-waste kitchen isn't just about saving money or reducing clutter--it's about reducing harm to our environment and prioritizing the health of our planet and its inhabitants.

Encourage farmer market visits

The journey to a zero-waste kitchen doesn't stop at your home's threshold. The sustainable practices and mindful consumption habits you cultivate within your kitchen can be carried forward into your community, influencing others and making a substantial and lasting impact on the environment at a larger scale. This process begins by adopting the role of an advocate for zero-waste living - promoting sustainable practices, educating others about the importance of waste reduction, and leading by example in the implementation of eco-conscious habits.

Engaging with your community can take on a myriad of forms, each with its own unique impact. Perhaps one of the simplest and most enjoyable ways of community engagement is patronizing your local farmers' market. A visit to the farmers' market is an excellent way to support your local economy, reduce carbon emissions associated with the transportation of goods, and most importantly, cut back on plastic waste.

Farmers' markets often sell produce without the plastic packaging found in typical supermarkets. Therefore, by bringing your reusable shopping bags, cloth produce bags, and glass containers for bulk items, you can easily avoid unnecessary waste. Additionally, the fresh produce you'll find at the farmers' market often outshines the quality found at conventional grocery stores. They are less likely to be waxed or chemically altered to prolong shelf-life, meaning you get to bring home goods just as nature intended, fresh, flavorful, and nourishing.

Farther than being mere shopping destinations, farmers' markets can also function as educational platforms. Engage with the farmers, learn about their farming processes, ask about their challenges and victories in the field. This knowledge not only enriches your understanding of the food you eat but can also arm you with valuable insights that you can share within your community to promote sustainable farming practices.

By making regular visits to farmers' markets a part of your routine, you're making a profound statement about the kind of food system you support and the types of practices you want to see sustained into the future. It's a commitment that radiates out from your zero-waste kitchen and touches the lives of the producers who grow your food, the community members who see you as an example, and ultimately, the health of the planet at large.

Remember, each effort, however small it may seem, has a ripple effect. By choosing to commit to zero-waste living and encouraging others to do the same, you have the power to spark immense change. Your zero-waste kitchen is not only a testament to your commitment to nurturing yourself and your loved ones but also a symbol of the respect and care you hold for your community and our shared world.

Contributing to Environmental Policy

Influence public waste management practices

Adopting the zero-waste lifestyle - especially in your kitchen - is not only a personal commitment to uphold sustainability; it also paves the way for you to become an advocate for zero-waste living. A zero-waste kitchen is more than a space that minimizes waste: it's a starting point for making broader and deeper impacts on a local, national, and global scale.

As an advocate, you become instrumental in shaping environmental policy. The call-to-action on reducing waste goes beyond educating friends, family, or local communities. We need to bring this message to the core group of decision-makers: our policy makers. The government has the power and the means to implement grander scale waste management practices that align with the philosophy of zero-waste living.

Involvement in creating effective environmental policy can take various forms, such as attending public hearings and town meetings, writing to your local representatives, or even serving on local boards and commissions. Policy influencing also involves being an active participant in the public consultations of proposed policies.

Another critical role to play is promoting and influencing the public's waste management activities. This endeavor requires a multi-faceted approach - engaging the community in discussions about the importance of waste reduction and introducing strategies on proper segregation, recycling, and composting. It requires proving the practicability of zero-waste living through initiatives like community composting, hosting zero-waste workshops, and spearheading local clean-ups.

Participation in these activities not only fosters community growth but also helps hone and shape environmental policies that cities, states, or even countries adhere to. Transforming your kitchen into a zero-waste haven is the first big step, but it doesn't, and it shouldn't, stop there. Advocate for large-scale change as you progress in your zero-waste journey. Remember, the ultimate goal extends beyond individual benefits towards the broader prize of global sustainability. And by becoming an advocate for zero-waste living, we can collectively turn the tide in favor of a cleaner, healthier, and waste-free Earth.

Contributing to environmental policy and influencing public waste management practices do not only involve grand gestures but also small, consistent efforts. As the saying goes, big things have small beginnings. By shifting our own behaviors and inspiring others to follow suit, we can influence policies - all from the cozy corners of our zero-waste kitchens.

Promote recycling and composting

The fundamental premise of cultivating a Zero-waste Kitchen isn't confined within the physical boundary of your home. Its implications and impact have a broad spectrum, extending from perishable produce to long-lasting kitchen appliances. Most importantly, these changes do not need to stay localized to personal kitchens. If utilized properly, they can echo into the community and even policy level changes.

Proponents of the Zero-waste Living movement understand their pivotal role as advocates. More and more citizens are getting active in their local communities, encouraging others to adopt sustainable habits, and emphasizing the importance of recycling, composting, and waste reduction that goes beyond mere personal changes.

Becoming an advocate for Zero-waste Living, however, requires more than an encyclopedia of knowledge. Commitment and action are equally, if not more, essential. It begins with familiarizing oneself with local waste management policies, recycling procedures and understanding the regulations surrounding waste disposal.

As advocates, it's necessary to know which materials can be recycled and which cannot. Exploring the potential of compostable waste to create nutrient-rich soil can redirect a significant amount of waste from landfills. Encouraging local businesses to do the same not only paves the way for a sustainable future but also presents an opportunity for economic growth.

Contribution to environmental policy is a more institutionalized way to make a change. Citizens can propose changes to current waste management legislation, promote the diversion of recyclables from landfills, and advocate for food waste reduction strategies within their local governments. Such strategies might include imposing tighter regulations on excess food waste by large corporations, implementing mandatory composting and recycling programs, or prohibiting single-use plastics.

An individual acting alone might significantly reduce their waste, but a community working together can revolutionize their entire waste system. Not only is this journey towards zero waste achievable, but it is also incredibly rewarding. It brings together community members, begins crucial conversations about sustainability, and conserves precious resources while doing so.

In order to develop a sustainable future, we need to go beyond treating symptoms and start addressing the root problems. Our waste issue isn't simply about needing better technologies to manage it. We need a societal shift - a different way of relating to the materials we use every day. This change starts in our kitchens, in our communities, and will gradually broadens to impact our policies and legislation.

Creating a Zero-waste Kitchen and becoming an advocate for the Zero-waste Living movement serves as a catalyst in ushering in an era of responsible consumption and effective waste management. Everyone has a role to play in this green revolution, let's start from where we are, one step at a time.

Participate in environmental law-making

In recent years, the idea of zero-waste living has gained considerable traction, demonstrating that it is not only an essential line of defense against environmental damage, but also a way to enhance one's quality of life and save money. As the pursuit of zero-waste becomes increasingly mainstream, every individual has an exciting opportunity to become a change-maker, transforming their kitchen as the starting point and later, their entire lifestyle.

Contributing to environmental policy can take many forms, depending on each person's capability and willingness to participate. It can be as simple as contributing to local clean-up initiatives or as profound as lobbying for green alternatives in your community or workplace.

But before diving into the world of environmental activism, understanding the principles of zero-waste living is crucial. These principles are the driving force behind a lifestyle that radically cuts back on your environmental impact and allows you to be an advocate for both your health and the health of our planet. They include rethinking your needs, refusing what you do not need, reducing what you do need, reusing what you consume, recycling what you cannot refuse, reduce or reuse, and rot (compost) the rest.

These 6R principles form the basis upon which you can build your advocacy and reshape your lifestyle. It starts in your kitchen, where most waste is created and where simple, effective changes can often make the most significant impact. In due course, you aim to create a kitchen that not only generates minimal waste but also inspires others to reconsider their habits and their roles in the state of our world.

As you begin implementing the principles of zero-waste in your life, you may start to engage in more informed discussions about environmental policy. You may find yourself eager to contribute to a larger conversation, advocating for laws, regulations, and initiatives that reinforce the zero-waste model. You could become involved in environmental law-making processes at various levels, influencing policy decisions that affect both personal and community waste management.

Your journey towards a zero-waste lifestyle, starting from transforming your kitchen into an eco-friendly haven, not only brings about a change in your personal lifestyle but potentially impacts the broader community, government policies, and global perspectives on waste management. As you progress on this path, remember that every action you take is a contribution to the overall global improvements we need to ensure a healthy and sustainable world for generations to come. Our journey to a zero-waste kitchen is the first step in this grand endeavor, an exalted manifestation of our responsibility and capacity as earth's stewards.

Support sustainable packaging initiatives

Becoming an advocate for zero-waste living is an essential and impactful journey that not only reforms your way of life but also influences those around you to reduce, reuse, and recycle. This decisive step begins within your kitchen, a space often swarming with expendable packaging and non-refillable containers. By assuming responsibility and making conscious choices, you can transform your cooking area into a sustainable and eco-friendly haven.

Beginning this journey requires a paradigm shift towards mindful consumption. It invites you to scrutinize the lifecycle of the items you purchase — from production and distribution to usage and disposal. The pack of chips you enjoy during movie nights, the canned beans making your recipes flavorful, or the plastic-wrapped vegetables in your refrigerator - each product has made a substantial journey before making it to your house. The cost of this journey is not just monetary but significantly environmental.

By making a commitment to zero-waste living, you endorse the reduce-reuse-recycle mantra, which necessitates placing emphasis on minimizing waste at its inception. Adopting this principle denotes a lifestyle overhaul beyond merely recycling. It's about simplifying needs, reducing demands, and changing consumption behaviors. Understanding this is crucial, as recycling, although imperative, does not remedy the complex problem of waste.

As consumers, we wield substantial power to influence market dynamics. If we consistently choose products with sustainable packaging, we send a strong message to manufacturers about our preferences. Eco-friendly choices eventually necessitate a shift in manufacturing norms, leading to less plastic-filled landfills and more recyclable, compostable, or reusable alternatives.

However, individual actions must be coupled with a robust framework of policies, standards, and laws. By maintaining our role as eco-conscious citizens and consumers, we can play a pivotal role in advocating and contributing to sound environmental policy. This includes campaigning for legislative changes, supporting policies targeting waste reduction, and advocating for businesses to adopt sustainable practices.

Simply put, adopting a zero-waste lifestyle implies advocating for a sustainable future. It may seem like small steps, such as choosing a cloth bag over plastic, or purchasing in bulk instead of individually packed items. But when aggregated, these steps evolve into a significant force for fostering sustainable practices in consumerism and manufacturing.

Towards this end, leveraging our collective strength as consumers and civil society allows us to vocalize the demand for environmentally friendly practices and products. It enables us to urge the business sector to foster innovation. And if our voices reverberate loudly enough, they must respond.

Remember, the shift to a zero-waste lifestyle begins at home, within our kitchens. And it doesn't just end there; it transcends into a wider sphere where our choices, voices, and actions catalyze systematic changes. Together, we hold the potential to protect our planet and create a sustainable future.

Contribute to green energy policies

Making a transition to a zero-waste kitchen is much more than just a personal lifestyle choice; it's a significant step towards advocating for sustainable living and contributing to an integral part of environmental policy. This book is not only aimed at providing practical steps for individuals and families to shift towards a waste-free cooking space but also acknowledges the importance of the larger conversation about environment protection and policy implementation.

Understanding the essence of zero-waste living often begins at a granular level, within our homes. However, it does not stop there. Changing our consumption, disposal habits, and culinary practices predicates a potential ripple effect on our immediate community, thereby contributing to the bigger conversation about sustainable living. This, however, is achieved not just through individual action, but by collaborating with others and advocating for systemic changes within our legislative structures and communities.

A critical contribution that we can offer is engaging actively with environmental policy creation and implementation. Policies are, in many ways, the backbone for any significant societal change. To facilitate a complete societal shift towards zero-waste, we need to ensure that our local, regional, and national policies are favorable towards the use of green energy alternatives and the recycling, reducing and reusing of resources.

Engagement with environmental policies can take multiple forms of action. This can involve anything from backing local initiatives, advocating for or against specific legislative proposals, or even running for a post in community bodies that have power over policy decisions. For instance, incentivization programs can be promoted for households adopting green energy solutions or stringent laws can be advocated for industries producing non-recyclable packaging.

Additionally, pushing for inclusive policies for green energy utilization is another noteworthy action. Green, renewable energy sources such as solar, wind, and geothermal are not only infinite but can substantially reduce our reliance on fossil fuels, which are the leading cause of greenhouse gas emissions. Green energy policies could ensure that these renewable sources become more accessible and affordable for the general population, further promoting sustainable living.

The journey towards a Zero-waste Kitchen, and more extensively, a zero-waste lifestyle, is not merely a personal quest but a collective effort. By leveraging our power as consumers, community members, and policy influencers, we can contribute significantly to both the tangible reduction of waste in our homes and the implementation of policy changes that favor environmental preservation.

In essence, your kitchen stands as an emblem of your commitment to sustainability – a commitment that extends far beyond the boundary of your home. As we proceed and delve deeper into making your kitchen an eco-friendly haven, remember that each step taken brings us collectively closer to fostering an environmentally friendly, sustainable world.

CONCLUSION

Reflections on the Journey

Acknowledging the accomplished transformation

The transformation of your kitchen to a zero-waste haven marks a significant milestone in your life – it acts as the first step towards adopting a sustainable lifestyle which not only benefits you but also our planet Earth. Reflecting on this journey brings attention to subtle shifts in habits which, over time, have now become second nature.

To begin this sustainable journey might have seemed like a herculean task but even the longest journey begins with a single step. Now when you look back, you realize this shift wasn't all that demanding or inconvenient. At the heart of it was a simple exercise of awareness - knowing what goes into our kitchen spaces, how it is used, and how it finally leaves. It might not have been a linear path, with its own twists and turns, a few lapses here and there, but it was a journey shaped by commitment, and more importantly, the willingness to make a difference.

Changes, big or small, toast to your resilience and dedication. Replacing plastic with eco-friendly alternatives, composting your kitchen waste, minimalizing wasteful habits, shopping locally, integrating minimalistic ideas, you have emerged a conscious consumer, a leader in your own right, fostering change directly or indirectly.

Moreover, the zero-waste kitchen has not been laborious but

rather therapeutic, feeding the body, nourishing the soul, restoring balance with nature. Each activity- be it sorting, recycling, reusing or composting, has been a meditative exercise, a process of quiet reflection, making your space and environment a haven of tranquility.

These transformations, while fundamentally rooted in your kitchen, have spread to other areas of your life too – influencing your choices, your decisions, and your general outlook towards life. That is the power of small but consistent actions – their effects ripple far beyond the visible.

Our kitchens, the heart of our homes, have now become a symbol of our commitment to our planet - embracing eco-friendly choices and promoting sustainability. This journey towards zero-waste is not merely a lifestyle trend, but a meaningful endeavour towards conserving our environment.

Remember, each step you've made towards building your zero-waste kitchen contributes to a much larger global impact on waste reduction. Celebrate your victories, spread the message, and keep pushing forward. This self-driven initiative has made you an ambassador of change who has the capability to inspire others on this journey. Be proud of the transformation you have accomplished and stay committed to your path.

In conclusion, your journey to creating a zero-waste kitchen is not the end, but the beginning of a sustainable lifestyle. Your kitchen is not just a cooking space anymore, it is your eco-friendly haven, a testament of your commitment to a sustainable future. After all, the journey to saving our planet starts at home.

Evaluating eco-friendly cooking habits

It has been quite the journey, delving into the world of eco-friendly kitchen practices, drawing back the veil to reveal the environmental impact of our daily actions. At first glance, transforming your kitchen into a zero-waste space may seem daunting, even unattainable. Yet, with a steadfast commitment to sustainable living, a sprinkle of self-education, and a dash of creativity, it's an achievable goal.

The primary objective of this book is to foster a shift in mindset towards more sustainable practices. You may initially define success as the complete eradication of waste in your kitchen. However, the process of moving to a zero-waste kitchen is indeed a journey, a constant evolution that alters the way we approach every aspect of our lives.

The journey teaches us that perfections isn't necessarily the goal. Reducing waste in the kitchen is a series of small, achievable steps. It involves evaluating our current habits and determining where we can make changes. It means no longer viewing things as disposable, but as resources with a lifecycle that we should respect and honor. Every step you take towards minimizing waste is a success in its own right.

Pause, sit back and look around your kitchen – you can notice changes, small or large. Maybe you now compost your food scraps or switched to reusable coffee filters–you're making a difference. Eco-friendly cooking habits not only reduce waste but are also budget-friendly and healthier.

A zero-waste kitchen helps us safeguard our environment, one meal at a time. This lifestyle promotes a healthier planet, a cleaner neighborhood, and a clear conscience. And rest assured, the transformation of your kitchen will most definitely ripple into other aspects of your life, igniting a broader passion for sustainability.

So even on days when you feel overwhelmed by this profound shift, remember that every little bit helps. Remember the three R's; Reduce, Reuse, and Recycle. Make them your mantra as you continue striving towards a greener future.

Always remember, this is a journey rather than a destination; continue to adapt and grow. Keep embracing practices that lower waste and seeking knowledge to sustain your eco-friendly cooking habits.

This is our chance to reverse some of the damage we've inflicted on our planet. We owe it to ourselves and the generations to come.

Thus, as we conclude, reflect on each step of your zero-waste journey. Evaluate your eco-friendly cooking habits regularly, and rest assured there's always more to learn, more to do. Pursuit of a zero-waste kitchen isn't just an end goal; it's a lifelong commitment to our planet's well-being. Together, we can make a difference, reducing waste one kitchen at a time.

Reflecting on waste reduction journey

Having taken the time to thoroughly explore the world of zero-waste in the context of our kitchens, it is now an appropriate moment to pause, reflect, and examine the journey we've embarked on together. Reducing waste, as we've come explored, is more than a superficial act of recycling or composting; it is an entire lifestyle change necessitating a shift of mindsets, routines, habits, and even shopping practices.

Applying the zero-waste philosophy in our kitchen is not without its challenges, from finding alternatives for disposable items to preparing meals ensuring minimal food waste, and consciously choosing products with less or no plastic packaging. However, witnessing the dramatic reduction in the amount of trash produced daily can strike a chord of remarkable accomplishment.

Consider the fact that the simplification of your cooking space can be seen as so much more than just decluttering. It's a step toward reclaiming control over what you consume, culminating in an intentional and fulfilling lifestyle. Imagining a world with fewer landfills and cleaner oceans is no longer a far-fetched ideal, but a potential reality that starts 'at home,' with you. And it's not only the environment that benefits from this transformation. An organized, less-filled, eco-friendly kitchen makes for a less cluttered and stress-filled mind.

Our goal for this journey was not strictly producing zero-waste, but appreciating the efforts and acts that decrease our waste contribution. It's about making conscious decisions and choices that aim towards a sustainable lifestyle. Through this book, you were provided with the tools to transform your kitchen, but more so, the power to transform your habits and perspectives towards waste and sustainability.

As we close this chapter, remember that the journey towards a zero-waste kitchen is a continuous cycle of learning, changing, and growing. It does not end here. Getting to the point of having a fully zero-waste kitchen may feel daunting or even impossible at first but remember: progress over perfection. The smallest changes, implemented consistently, have the potential to yield significant results in the long term.

In conclusion, this journey reinforces the notion that sustainability isn't a binary system where you're either 'good or bad' for the environment. Instead, it's a spectrum, and we're all collectively moving towards a more conscientious, sustainable future, one decision at a time. As per the adage of zero-waste lifestyle enthusiast Bea Johnson, "We can't do all the good that the world needs, but the world needs all the good that we can do." May your journey into a zero-waste kitchen inspire further sustainable changes within your home, your community, and indeed, our precious world.

Appreciating mindful consumption practices

As we reach the final pages of this insightful journey, it is imperative we take a moment to reflect on the transformative concepts we've explored throughout this comprehensive guide. Venturing into the unknown territory of a zero-waste kitchen can be a daunting feat but remember, every small effort counts and gradually leads to momentous changes.

For some, this transition into the eco-conscious way of life is instantaneous, prompted by a striking revelation. For others, it is gradual and unfolds over time. Regardless of the methods you employ or the pace at which you progress, the crux lies in your intention - your determination to reform your kitchen into a more sustainable, more earth-conscientious place.

Revamping your kitchen into a zero-waste haven is no fleeting fad or fashionable trend. It's a lifestyle choice, a conscious commitment towards waste reduction, resource optimization, and mindful consumption. Therefore, we must understand and appreciate the ethos underlying these practices - the enormous potential they possess to instigate powerful shifts in consumption patterns, waste management methodologies, and food habits.

The broad spectrum of measures available - from ditching plastic storage containers for glass jars, composting left-over kitchen scraps, preserving seasonal produce, to meal planning, and proper recycling- imbibing these practices can be a gradual progression or an immediate overhaul, and each step you take towards this direction brings you a step closer in achieving a zero-waste kitchen.

The overall experience of revamping your kitchen extends far beyond what's tangible and material. You will learn to appreciate the value and scarcity of resources, the impactful role you play in the broader ecological cycle, and the satisfaction derived from adopting a lifestyle that is symbiotic with nature. Moreover, your zero-waste kitchen may inspire others around you to venture on a similar path, thereby encouraging a chain of environmentally conscious transformations.

Remember, the journey to zero-waste is not one of perfection, but progression. As you gracefully navigate through this journey, let each milestone – no matter how trivial it may seem – serve as a celebration of your contribution to a healthier planet. Embrace the challenges, appreciate your efforts, and cherish the beautiful transformation that you've begun to unfold in your kitchen and in your life.

Above all, let the essence of mindful consumption practices percolate into every aspect of your life. Let this journey change not just your kitchen, but your interaction with all resources. Because 'Zero-waste' is not a destination, but a mindful journey towards a sustainable lifestyle – a finer way of living. Change starts at home, and what better place to initiate this change than the heart of your home – your kitchen. So, let's roll up our sleeves, continue to experiment with sustainable practices, adopt new habits, discard old ones, and strive towards cutting down our kitchen waste to zero.

Remember, each tiny step counts as a giant leap towards a sustainable world. Carry forth this changed perspective in every step you take and continue to inspire others to join the quest towards zero-waste. Together, we have the potential to make a difference. A significant, impactful, long-standing difference. Let's make our kitchens witness this transformation and be the torchbearers of change, conservation, and thoughtful consumption for our planet. Let's journey towards Zero-waste.

Looking ahead: continuous eco-innovation

After journeying through the principles, strategies, and practices of transforming your kitchen into a zero-waste haven, we now approach the closure of this enlightening voyage. Indeed, the journey has provided insights into more sustainable, eco-friendly ways of managing our kitchen activities, transforming our cooking spaces into eco-friendly havens, and significantly reducing our environmental footprints.

However, it's important to note that establishing a zero-waste kitchen goes beyond merely following the strategies and principles outlined in this guide. It is about fostering a paradigm shift in our relationship with food, packaging, waste, and the environment. It entails cultivating a respectful, considerate relationship with nature and its resources. This transformation should resonate beyond our kitchens, permeating other areas of our lives, especially in how we consume resources and manage waste.

The journey to a zero-waste kitchen doesn't stop at the final pages of this book, as it is a continuous process of self-education, experimentation, and improvement. As the zero-waste movement continues to gather momentum globally, novel solutions and techniques to waste reduction will inevitably emerge, calling for continuous eco-innovation. Seize every opportunity to stay updated with such advancements, striving always to implement new solutions whenever possible - every action counts.

Reflect on your journey thus far. What changes have you implemented? What achievements have made you proud? Are there areas that seem challenging? Use these reflections not as a tool to judge progress, but as an ally to improve and innovate continuously.

Looking ahead, the hope is not only for you to perpetuate these practices but also for you to inspire others to incorporate these principles into their lifestyles. Share your knowledge and experience with family, friends, and your wider community. Remember, small actions can have significant impacts when multiplied across many households.

A zero-waste kitchen is attainable, as demonstrated throughout this guide. However, the transition requires time, patience, effort, and above all, perseverance. Remember, every step towards sustainability counts and is worth celebrating. Let your zero-waste journey be an engaging, fulfilling, and transformative process, continuously evolving as we strive to make better choices for the environment. Keep this book handy, refer back to it, extract from it, absorb it and continue the invaluable venture towards a zero-waste lifestyle within and beyond the kitchen.

The journey we embarked on together through these pages is the beginning of more eco-conscious and zero-waste endeavors at large. Keep the passion burning, retain the momentum and remember, each one of us plays a crucial role in shaping a more sustainable, greener future. Happy zero-wasting!

Inspiration for Continuing the Practice

Sustaining an environmentally supportive lifestyle

The journey towards a zero-waste kitchen is not one that happens overnight. It is rather a continuous process of understanding, learning, adaptation, and most importantly, commitment. And the culmination of this journey is not the end; it's the beginning of going beyond confines, incorporating more sustainable practices, and establishing a truly eco-friendly haven.

Embracing a zero-waste lifestyle invariably involves making changes that go far beyond the kitchen. The steps you have taken in your kitchen can be the launching pad for broader scale changes in other aspects of your life. What starts with composting food scraps or substituting plastic containers with glass ones can lead to comprehensive waste management for the entire house, growing your own food, or even becoming an advocate for renewable energy.

What is essential to realize is that the road to zero-waste kitchen is not a solitary journey. You are part of a worldwide movement of people who are concerned about the environment and are taking steps to minimize the harm they cause to it. Connecting with this larger community can provide both inspiration and practical tips. You may find local groups that share your interest or online communities where you can exchange ideas and experiences.

Moreover, it's critical to celebrate even the smallest milestones along the way. Remember, every single step towards minimizing waste contributes valiantly to the preservation of our planet. No action in this regard is too meager. What ultimately matters are persistence and the unyielding determination to continue the practice.

Lastly, take a breather and relish the satisfaction gained from living a lifestyle that's beneficial not just for you but for generations to come. As you have progressed on this journey, you will have realized that a zero-waste lifestyle doesn't only generate environmental benefits but also positives for your personal life. Be it financial savings accrued from reducing waste, health gains from consuming fresh produce, or the sheer peace of mind achieved from knowing that your actions are helping the world become a better place, the benefits are numerous and all-encompassing.

The wonderful aspect of the zero-waste lifestyle rests with its fluidity and flexibility. It's a personal journey that permits evolution and growth. Armed with knowledge and passion, you have all the tools to transform your kitchen – and potentially your lifestyle – into the epitome of sustainability. And always remember, this journey is accompanied by remarkable strength; the more people practice it around the globe, every small initiative adds up to a massive global impact.

To conclude, keep innovating, experimenting and learning. The road to sustainability is wide open for exploration. Venture onto this exciting path and let it lead you to unexpected avenues of environmental stewardship. Keep striving, keep progressing, and continue to set novel, inspiring examples for the world to follow. Sustainability is no longer just an option; it's the only way forward, and your zero-waste kitchen is a monumental step in the right direction.

Actively pursuing kitchen waste reduction

After coming this far, one may appreciate the fact that establishing a zero-waste kitchen is more fundamental than just refusing, reducing, and recycling; it goes beyond these ritual practices. It is about a shift in mindset that integrates environmentally friendly habits into our daily routine, a conscious decision that grows into a lifestyle change. It is about being cognizant of our consumption habits and making responsible choices not just for ourselves, but for the community and the environment.

A zero-waste kitchen might be a daunting endeavor, especially for the uninitiated. The task is undoubtedly an ongoing one and might seem overwhelming at times. In the initial stages, progress might feel slow; however, it's crucial to remember that every small step leads us closer to our ultimate goal. Hence, it's essential to take heart in the little victories and continue refining your habits and strategies to make your cooking space greener, leaner, and cleaner every day.

The essence of a zero-waste kitchen is that it encourages us to think globally and act locally. Every meal we create, every ingredient we purchase, and every utensil we use are opportunities for making a difference. By refusing to use disposable items, reducing our waste, reusing containers, recycling materials, and composting food scraps, we are positively influencing various environmental factors, including reducing air and water pollution, preserving natural resources, conserving energy, and decreasing the environmental footprint significantly.

We encourage you to derive inspiration from the many case studies we have included in this book, people who have successfully created a sustainable and Eco-friendly kitchen from scratch, many starting with no prior knowledge or exposure to zero-waste practices. Read their stories, absorb their wisdom, and let it motivate you to continue on your unique journey of transformation.

Always remember, transforming your kitchen into a zero-waste haven is not merely a short-term goal, it's a lifetime commitment. It requires persistent effort, continuous learning, and undeterred commitment. As you embark on or continue this journey, let your kitchen tell a story of respect, for our planet, our health, and our future generations. Defining our relationships with the environment on your terms offers a mindfulness that stretches far beyond the kitchen's confines into all areas of life.

In conclusion, cutting kitchen waste is more than just a noble initiative; it's an urgent necessity for the world we live in today. The process provides us with a chance to revitalize our kitchen space, re-think our consumption habits, and re-define our relationship with the environment. Let us move forward together, one step at a time, one day at a time, with the hope that our consistent efforts will lead to a healthier planet and a sustainable future for all.

Reiterating benefits of zero-waste

As we reach the conclusion of this comprehensive guide, it is pivotal to reflect on why the transformation towards zero-waste is not only essential but also impactful in shaping our cooking space into an eco-friendly haven. The journey towards constructing a zero-waste kitchen, as detailed through this guide, is not merely about waste reduction. Rather, it's about cultivating a mindset committed to sustainability, fostering responsibility towards the environment, and ultimately fostering a better world — one meal, one day, and one kitchen at a time.

The benefits that come forward with the adoption of a zero-waste practice in our kitchen are endless, touching not only our lives but also the generations to come. This eco-friendly lifestyle is capable of saving numerous resources in the process. From saving money by purchasing only necessary items and reducing food waste, streamlining your meals and creating a more efficient kitchen - the benefits are far-reaching. It contributes significantly to mitigating climate change by reducing our individual carbon footprints. Indeed, the act of transforming our kitchen into a zero-waste space ventures beyond our culinary pursuits, it is about influencing change on a grand scale.

The path of zero-waste may seem challenging at the beginning, filled with the pressure of eradicating waste entirely. However, remember that the core of this practice is gradual transformation and improvement rather than perfection. Every small step towards the reduction of waste accumulates into a larger feat. So, whether it's through composting food waste, cooking with seasonal and local produce, embracing reusable products, or simply striving for meal preparation without waste - every action holds value.

Your journey toward a zero-waste kitchen has the potential

to inspire those around you. You carry a great power influence which can affect your family, friends, and even complete strangers when sharing your positive experiences and challenges. The goal is for every kitchen to become an eco-friendly haven, and your story can be the starting point for many others.

Let this detailed guide be an inspiration for your continuous journey towards sustainability. Let it serve as a blueprint, a source of ideas, and a helpful companion as you continue to experiment and learn. We encourage you to continue exploring, innovating, being consistent, and above all, believing in the positive impact your actions exert on our wonderful world.

In summary, transforming your kitchen into a zero-waste haven is a rewarding journey full of invaluable learning experiences. The process may seem daunting at first, but with dedication, experimentation, and patience, it becomes a fulfilling practice. So, keep taking strides toward this eco-friendly lifestyle, carry the inspiration you've gained from this book, and continue to affect change - one kitchen at a time.

Continual modification of eco-habits

In conclusion, the concept of a Zero-waste Kitchen is not solely a trend to be adopted momentarily, but rather, a lifestyle adjusting internal compass that aligns with a sustainable world. The journey to becoming more eco-friendly within your kitchen environment doesn't end on the last page of this guide but should inspire a continuing practice that seeps into all other aspects of your life.

The essence of a kitchen producing zero-waste isn't just about recycling more regularly or using biodegradable alternatives, it's about a shift in mindset. It's about viewing waste not as a disposable problem but as an opportunity to reduce what we bring into our homes in the first place. Once you have made these changes, applied the principles, and seen the transformation, there is a sense of accomplishment and satisfaction that will inspire ongoing commitment.

Continual modification of eco-habits is the key to maintaining a Zero-waste Kitchen. Beyond what is taken to heart from this guide, it is important to stay updated on new technologies, alternatives, and recycling programs that continually emerge. Our world keeps evolving, and so should our habits. The goal is not perfection, but creating a sustainable system that adapts and grows with you. Chasing perfection might deter you from the path, while accepting that there are lapses, and the most important thing is to keep improving and refining.

Providing yourself the permissible leniency to adapt these practices at your pace will prevent the journey from becoming overwhelming. Just as with any new practice, it will take time for these suggestions to become second nature, but persistence will soon make these green habits a part of your lifestyle.

In summary, the Zero-waste Kitchen is much more than

a sustainable means of living; it's a lifetime commitment towards minimizing waste and maximizing eco-friendly efforts. It's about making small but impactful changes that will not only transform your cooking space but will foster an enduring commitment to a more sustainable global community.

Inspiring others through action

In embracing the ethos of a zero-waste kitchen, we not only cultivate an environment that encourages sustainability, but we also imbue our daily routines with purpose and intention, understanding that each step we take makes a difference. However, the journey towards a zero-waste kitchen doesn't end with the implementation of eco-friendly practices in our own homes. It extends beyond our personal spaces, influencing those within our sphere and inspiring further change.

One of the most profound impacts of adopting a zero-waste lifestyle is that it plants a seed of environmental consciousness that can inspire others. As we navigate this path and reap the benefits of being eco-conscious consumers, we become ambassadors for this cause, with the ability to influence and inspire those around us. The simplicity of a well-structured, eco-friendly kitchen has the potential to captivate the attention of our friends, our families, and our broader social circles, setting a ripple effect into motion.

Our cooking spaces are intimate, personal areas which exhibit our lifestyle choices. Thus, by transforming them into eco-friendly havens, we exemplify the practicality and effectiveness of a sustainable lifestyle. Naturally, this will trigger curiosity and interest among those who witness this transformation.

Sharing our experiences and the tangible rewards of a zero-waste kitchen is an excellent way to inspire onlookers. Let's illustrate the benefits and empower each other with the knowledge and methods that make this transition possible and beneficial. By sharing our journey, we can demystify any misconceptions about it being tedious or expensive. Instead, we can highlight how it can save money, decrease clutter, improve health, and provide immense satisfaction of contributing to a greener planet.

The adoption of a zero-waste lifestyle in our kitchens starts with us – but it doesn't have to end with us. After implementing these changes, we become more than users of a zero-waste kitchen. We become advocates for zero-waste practices, inspiring others to follow suit in their cooking spaces and promoting a more sustainable lifestyle. The journey toward sustainability in our kitchen is a proactive step toward fostering a globally eco-conscious community.

The principles of a zero-waste kitchen go beyond saving resources or reducing waste. It's about identifying our role in the planet's health and making conscious decisions that carry significant implications. This transformative journey encourages personal growth, community support, and a sense of belonging in an eco-conscious globe. As we adapt and evolve, let our kitchens be more than spaces for cooking food. Let them be catalysts for environmental consciousness, and let our actions inspire others to embark on this journey of sustainability.

In conclusion, creating a zero-waste kitchen is more than an end goal. It's a continuous process that inspires us and has the potential to motivate families, friends, and the world at large. Let us remember that the journey towards a zero-waste kitchen beams much farther than our homes. Its true power lies in the inspiration it provides for others, catalyzing a chain reaction towards a sustainable world. The zero-waste journey doesn't end with us; it begins with us.

Final Thoughts

Emphasizing sustainability's importance

The journey towards creating a zero-waste kitchen is a progressive one, which does not merely end with the implementation of sustainable habits. Rather, it is a continuous process of learning, growing and adapting to new ideas and methods that promote environmental conservation. As with any major lifestyle change, it is pertinent to remember that the key to success lies in consistency and commitment.

The underlying principle of managing a zero-waste kitchen is simplicity. It goes beyond just an eco-friendly approach to cooking. It fundamentally alters the way we perceive consumption and food management, urging us to be more conscious and thoughtful consumers. By proactively minimizing waste, repurposing leftovers, and making sustainable buying choices, we take significant steps towards reducing our individual carbon footprints.

However, it is crucial to note that the concept of a zero-waste kitchen is influenced by several factors including lifestyle, budget, local accessibility to sustainable products, and personal values. Not everyone may be able to attain absolute zero-waste, and that's okay. It's not about perfection, but rather progression.

As we conclude this comprehensive guide, let us emphasize that sustainability's importance cannot be overstated. We live in a time where the well-being of our environment has never been more perilous, where our daily decisions carry the potential to enact real change. The initiative to switch to an eco-friendly kitchen might seem like a microcosm in the larger scheme, but its cumulative effect is huge.

Every zero-waste kitchen contributes to a greener, healthier planet. It is an affirmation that we are conscious of our roles as responsible stewards of Nature. It may start with replacing plastic containers with glass jars or composting kitchen waste, but it ultimately leads to a broader awareness and understanding of our consumption habits.

In the grand tableau of sustainability, a zero-waste kitchen is but a single brush stroke. Yet, each kitchen, each choice, each conscious action, unites to create a distinct, collective impact. As we transform our cooking spaces into eco-friendly havens, we inspire others and ourselves to rethink perception towards waste and sustainability.

Let's remember, the goal is not just to create an impact, but to foster a legacy – starting from our kitchens, reverberating throughout our lives, and stretching outwards to influence the world. On this note, let us proceed in our quests for an environmentally sound and sustainable future. Your zero-waste kitchen is not just a concept but a commendable stride in the marathon for a sustainable lifestyle. Keep learning, keep reducing, keep reusing and most importantly, keep recycling. Let us remember, every granule of effort counts.

Encouraging conscious consumption

In conclusion, the movement towards a zero-waste kitchen is far more than a mere trend—it is a lifestyle choice and commitment. It represents a conscientious shift towards sustainable living, responsible conservation of our natural resources, mindfully minimizing our carbon footprint, and contributing to maintaining a healthier planet. By embracing these steps outlined in this book, you have taken the first significant stride towards an eco-friendly kitchen.

The elimination of waste in our kitchens is a journey of continuous effort and evolution. The transformation will not occur overnight. Each small task, each deliberate action, accumulates over time to create a substantial impact. It sets the course for a more sustainable lifestyle that goes beyond the confines of your cooking space spreading into other aspects of everyday living.

Each one of us has a vital role to play in this global movement towards sustainability. In our daily routines and habits, we can make subtle shifts and adaptations that cater not just to our needs but also respect the balance of our landscape. We may not realize but the simple and daily acts of preparing our meals, storing and disposing of our food, can be significant sources of waste. Altering these small bits of our routine helps reduce the burden of waste enormously.

Remember, the zero-waste kitchen is not about perfection; it's about making better, more mindful choices. A zero-waste lifestyle doesn't happen all at once, every small change contributes to a massive shift. It's about choosing to live a life that is sustainable—one that will allow our planet to sustain its own life as well.

Let this book be your guide in your journey towards a zero-waste kitchen. Practice and incorporate these strategies one at a time and soon enough, these would seamlessly blend into your daily lifestyle. Recognize it as not just a single person's endeavor but an investment in the environment and thereby a healthier future for the ones to follow.

Conscious consumption is not just a decision; it's a way of life. Invest time and effort in understanding the food you consume, where it comes from, and how it impacts the environment. Select locally sourced and seasonal produce, prioritize reusable over disposable items, and most importantly, make mindful decisions.

Everything begins at home. With this knowledge, you are now equipped with the tools and strategies to transform your kitchen into an eco-friendly haven. It's about making enduring changes, even if they seem small and insignificant in the beginning. It's about embracing a lifestyle that values sustainability over convenience. With every small step, you'll be contributing significantly to a more sustainable world.

So, here's to a healthier planet, a minimalistic lifestyle, and a zero-waste kitchen that encourages conscious consumption. The journey is just as vital as the destination. Take it one step at a time, persist, and most importantly, remember: every bit counts. Make the change, inspire others to follow suit, and together let's help bring about the transformation we want to see in the world.

Promoting waste-free practices

The journey we have embarked upon in reducing waste in our kitchen environment isn't just about saving money or making the most of our ingredients, it is inherently about contributing towards a greener future and creating a sustainable planet. The choices we make in our homes, in particular our kitchens, can immensely influence our environmental footprint and lead to substantial change.

From initial steps like composting and reevaluating our shopping habits, to more extensive tasks such as mindful meal planning and innovative cooking techniques, we have explored the multitude of ways through which we can transform our cooking space into an eco-friendly haven. It is equally important to remember that zero-waste endeavor is not about perfection, but about making better, more sustainable choices whenever possible.

As we conclude this comprehensive guide, the takeaway is to understand that every small measure counts when it comes to implementing zero-waste practices. It may seem insignificant to save a scrap of vegetable or a piece of cling film, but consistent mindfulness in our everyday actions can create significant shifts in our waste production. Through time and continual practice, this lifestyle can then become a habit, streamlining an eco-conscious existence with everyday living.

The change needs not to be drastic, let it be gradual. It's more important that we make ample room for learning, understanding, and adaptation. In due time, mistakes and mishaps will transform into a foundation for a better and a much more sustainable way of life.

Reflecting upon the path we have outlined here, we can apply these methods and concepts not just confined to our kitchen space. The underlying philosophy of zero-waste—

reuse, repurpose, and recycle—can guide us in every other aspect of our lives, widening the scope of sustainability beyond something as specific as kitchen waste.

Finally, promoting these waste-free practices within our friend circles, family members, and the wider society can have a profound impact. Let's be the ambassadors of a lifestyle that encourages the preservation of our planet. Creating sustainable kitchens is a step towards a sustainable world – let's make it a global strategy rather than an isolated practice.

Remember, zero-waste is not just a goal, it's a journey. And every journey begins with a single step. You have already taken that first step by exploring this guide. May this serve as a reliable resource in your quest to build a truly zero-waste kitchen, and a sustainable life. Here's to our shared commitment to make the world a better, healthier, and pollution-free place!

Underlining kitchen-specific strategies

As we draw the curtains on our exploration of the Zero-waste Kitchen concept, it is important to underline specific strategies that apply uniquely to the kitchen environment. These are not just mere blueprints but consistent action points that must be implemented with conscious and deliberate effort.

Firstly, the incorporation of bulk buying, which simply means purchasing food items in large quantities to reduce packaging waste. This is not only cost-effective but also reduces the frequency of shopping, hence leading to lesser consumption of fuel. In making this transition, one must be wary of purchasing perishable items in bulk to avoid food waste due to spoilage. Opt, instead, for pantry staples with longer shelf lives like rice, pasta, and legumes.

Secondly, plan your meals in advance. Having a meal plan helps in grocery shopping and ensures you buy only what you need, consequently reducing food waste. It also aids in avoiding packaged foods that are tempting to buy for last-minute meals.

Next is composting. Composting is the natural process of recycling organic waste into a rich soil conditioner. It not only reduces the need for chemical fertilizers but also aids in reducing landfill waste. Invest in a compost bin for your kitchen scraps, and you will be amazed at how much waste you will divert from the landfill.

Remember also to incorporate the culture of utilizing left-over food. Leftovers, if properly stored, can serve as meals for another day or transformed into a completely new dish. This step reduces the amount of food waste generated in the kitchen.

Lastly, consider investing in reusable products such as

beeswax wraps, silicone storage bags, and cloth napkins. They may cost more upfront, but they last for years and will save money in the long run. Reusables are healthier for the environment and reduce the amount of plastic that ends up in our ocean and landfills.

Adopting a sustainable, zero-waste lifestyle in the kitchen not only harmonizes our cooking space with nature but also enhances our personal life quality. It cultivates an attitude of resourcefulness, creativity, and respect for the environment, heralding a paradigm shift from the throw-away culture to a lifestyle that embraces and preserves our planet.

Creating a zero-waste kitchen is an ongoing journey, not a race or a finish line, so it's important to be patient with oneself in the process. Everyone's zero-waste journey will look different. However, the collective outcome would be significant in creating an eco-friendly haven in our kitchens and playing our part in maintaining the health and survival of our planet. The zero-waste kitchen is indeed not just a concept, but a lifestyle that is highly achievable and rewarding.

Reiterating lifelong benefits

In wrapping up, let's distill the concept of a zero-waste kitchen into its core. What we are dealing with is not just a kitchen, but a symbol of our commitment to a better, healthier, and sustainable environment. The actions we initiate in our cooking spaces reverberate beyond their walls, carrying an impact that affects our household, our community, and eventually the world at large.

A zero-waste kitchen, as the term suggests, merges the art of cooking with the principles of sustainability. It strips wasteful practices bare, replacing them with eco-friendly habits rooted in respect for our natural resources and conscious consumerism. This comprehensive guide has aimed to provide you with all the tools and knowledge necessary to embark on this transformative journey.

However, it is essential to remember that the transition to a zero-waste kitchen is not a one-size-fits-all process. What works for one household may not work for another. The beauty of this journey lies in its adaptability and the limitless room it provides for customized solutions.

The benefits of transforming your cooking space into a zero-waste haven are manifold. Firstly, it alleviates the strain on our environment by reducing waste and plastic pollution. We contribute to a circular economy wherein resources are utilized to their fullest extent possible, and waste is essentially designed out of the system.

Secondly, a zero-waste kitchen is likely to have a positive impact on our wallets. By cutting down on packaged goods, investing in reusable materials, and adopting mindful practices like meal planning, bulk shopping, and preserving leftovers, we can save substantial amounts of money over time.

Thirdly, embarking on this journey often entails embracing healthier food choices. Homemade meals, fermented foods, and fresh ingredients are hallmarks of a zero-waste kitchen as they come without the excess packaging. The resulting diet is thus naturally leaner, richer in nutrients, and absent of the harmful additives commonly found in processed foods.

Lastly, the journey is remarkably empowering. There is a unique sense of satisfaction and fulfilment in taking active steps to reduce one's environmental footprint. Devising solutions, adopting new practices, influencing others in the process - all these facets contribute to a heightened sense of purpose.

As the curtain falls on the guide, let's not view this as an ending, but as a precursor to new beginnings. The zero-waste kitchen is inherently a practice of constant learning, unlearning, and relearning. Our world is dynamic, and our strategies to protect it likewise need to evolve continually. With each change, each effort, no matter how small, we contribute to a better future – for ourselves, for future generations, and for our planet.

Remember, your journey towards a zero-waste kitchen doesn't end with the last page of this book. Instead, it flourishes with every meal you prepare, every mason jar you refill, and every packaging material you choose to forego. The road to sustainability is not always easy, but every step taken in the right direction leaves a footprint for others to follow.

Here's to our shared journey towards a sustainable future. One kitchen at a time.